TOM HIRSCHFELD,

author of the bestselling

HOW TO MASTER THE VIDEO GAMES,

zapped America with secret strategies for the 30 most popular arcade video games.

AND NOW...

16 most popular video games of the new billion-dollar national pastime invade your home!

HERE IS THE REVOLUTIONARY NEW 9-STEP METHOD FOR LEARNING

HOW TO MASTER HOME VIDEO GAMES!

Bantam Books by Tom Hirschfeld

HOW TO MASTER THE VIDEO GAMES
HOW TO MASTER HOME VIDEO GAMES

HOW TO MASTER HOME VIDEO GAMES

by
Tom Hirschfeld

Originated by
Roberta Grossman
and
Walter Zacharius

BANTAM BOOKS
Toronto New York London Sydney

HOW TO MASTER HOME VIDEO GAMES

A Bantam Book / March 1982

SPACE INVADERS, ASTEROIDS, WARLORDS, MISSILE COMMAND, COMBAT and PAC-MAN are trademarks of Atari, Inc.

SEA BATTLE, ARMOR BATTLE, ASTROSMASH, SPACE ARMADA and SPACE BATTLE are trademarks of Mattel Electronics.

DRAGSTER, KABOOM!, FREEWAY, LASER BLAST and STAMPEDE are trademarks of Activision, Inc.

ADVENTURE is a trademark of Atari, Inc.

Illustrated by Dusan Krajan, Tony Cinquina, Yook Louie and Raman Patel

Cover photograph by
Douglas C. Looney

ISBN 0-553-20195-6

Published simultaneously in the United States and Canada

Bantam Books are published by Bantam Books, Inc. Its trademark, consisting of the words "Bantam Books" and the portrayal of a rooster, is Registered in U.S. Patent and Trademark Office and in other countries. Marca Registrada. Bantam Books, Inc., 666 Fifth Avenue, New York, New York 10103.

PRINTED IN THE UNITED STATES OF AMERICA

0 9 8 7 6 5 4 3 2 1

THANKS

My thanks to Tony Armstrong, David Crane, Shawn Dybdahl, Roberta Grossman, Julie Herman, Alan Hirschfeld, John Hirschfeld, Leonard Hirschfeld, Phyllis Hirschfeld, Chuck Hunter Sr., Dale Hunter, Jack Looney, Steve Marmel, Robert Merek, Hing Ng, Brian Press, Jay Press, Bob Reynolds, Douglas Rochler, Todd Rogers, Andy Rosenbaum, Steve Rosenbaum, Mike Smithson, Frank Tetro, Ken Vance, and Walter Zacharius, and to Bill Heineman, the video gamer's video gamer.

CONTENTS

INTRODUCTION

Video games, both home and coin operated, are sweeping America and the world. Since the advent of Atari's PONG in 1972, we have been amazed by the new-found ability to **interact** with our TV sets. Home video games have magically transformed an instrument of passive enjoyment into a limitless competitive wonderland, a fantasy world in which family members can test their skills and endurance, participating alone, in teams, or in friendly rivalry. With the recent overwhelming surge in popularity of arcade video games, nearly everyone knows of such diabolical machines as SPACE INVADERS, ASTEROIDS, and PAC-MAN. The future for video games seems bright.

My last book, **How To Master The Video Games,** concerned mainly the coin-operated variety. I have been happy to hear from players whose scores that book has improved; others have asked me when someone would write a book on strategies for home video games. Eventually, I decided to attempt a simple explanation of such games in book form, hoping to save players whatever confusion and frustration I could.

With help from my friends and from home video manufacturers, who put me in touch with national champions and even game designers, I evolved a system for mastering any game quickly and efficiently, for it seems that many players do not learn the games in the simplest and most comprehensive way. The book also includes in-depth analyses of 15 games, the five best-selling strategy cartridges from each of the three leading manufacturers, Atari, Intellivision, and Activision. Each of the game sections uses the same format:

1. Diagram of the screen with all parts labeled
2. Explanation of the controls
3. Explanation of the scoring system

4. Explanation of direct threats to the player—which occurrences will end the game
5. Observations about the game
6. Strategies, from the obvious to the subtle, derived from all the information above

In addition to a brief technical chapter, I have included a discussion of Atari, Mattel, Activision, and other American manufacturers. Another chapter shows exercises for improving skills, such as peripheral vision and hand-eye coordination, that all the games require. Then follow lists of official records in the 15 games and the clubs for players. You can also read a whimsical bit of home video lore entitled "The Case of the Proud Programmer."

The principles of arcade games are often similar to those of home video, so there is a short survey of today's coin-operated games. For players who would like to get in touch with manufacturers, the book concludes with a list of their names, addresses, and telephone numbers.

The more seriously you decide to play any game, the better are the chances that you will master it. Keep in mind, though, that home video offers two equally important goals; one may be to score high, but the other is to enjoy yourself.

1

FOR BEGINNERS ONLY

If you are a newcomer to the world of video games, you should familiarize yourself with some of their common characteristics. Home video is initially slightly more demanding than arcade video because of all the various components–console, cartridge, controller, adapter, TV, and so on. Many similarities between the two types do exist, however.

Every home video game, for example, includes some type of maneuvering by the player, accomplished by the use of keyboards, dials, or joysticks. After reading the Controls section of a game strategy, you will understand immediately your potential for maneuvering in that game.

Most games use one or more FIRE buttons. Except when the Observations section states differently, the player's spaceship, plane, tank, or other representative fires in the direction it is facing. Games such as MISSILE COMMAND and SEA BATTLE use cursors, or target markets, instead. The player's enemies, when hit, explode and disappear without a trace except as noted in ASTEROIDS, COMBAT, ARMOR BATTLE, and others.

Games end after the time runs out, one player wins, or the supply of ships, tanks, planes, and whatever is used up. The player always has one of two objectives: scoring points or finishing in minimum time.

This effort may involve shooting as many enemies or reacting to dangers as quickly as possible. Enemies often appear in "screens" that must be annihilated before the next screen appears. Other names for screens, depending on the game, are "rounds," "points," "groups," or "waves." One fact, however, holds true for most of the games: the better you play them, the harder they can become.

2

KNOW YOUR ENEMY

A home video expert doesn't have to be a computer whiz, but a rudimentary understanding of your system's insides never hurts if you want to master the outside. When you are analyzing the way a cartridge "thinks," you should know at least a little about the form of its "brain."

The typical game system consists of the owner's television set, a TV/GAME switch box that connects to the set's VHF terminals, a console connected to the switch box; and two or more handheld controllers connected to the console. This apparatus is called the "hardware," whereas the game cartridges themselves are known as "software."

The following diagram represents the interaction between the software and the hardware during play. Schematically, "input" refers to your actions at the controls; what you do is relayed instantly to tiny silicon chips known as microprocessors. The game uses two types of recall, Random Access Memory (RAM) and Read Only Memory (ROM). The RAM retains temporary data such as the score and the number of ships, tanks, buckets, or whatever that you have left. The ROM, however, never alters; it keeps permanent information such as the rules of the game, that is, the program, which is usually written in assembler language.

Many programs use a Random Event Generator (REG). The REG prevents you from guessing when and where your next enemy will appear, for example, or what configurations your battleground will assume.

So, your actions are fed into the microprocessors, which use them and the RAM and ROM to produce the output that appears on the screen microseconds later. The more you know about how cartridges think, the better you can analyze and master any cartridge.

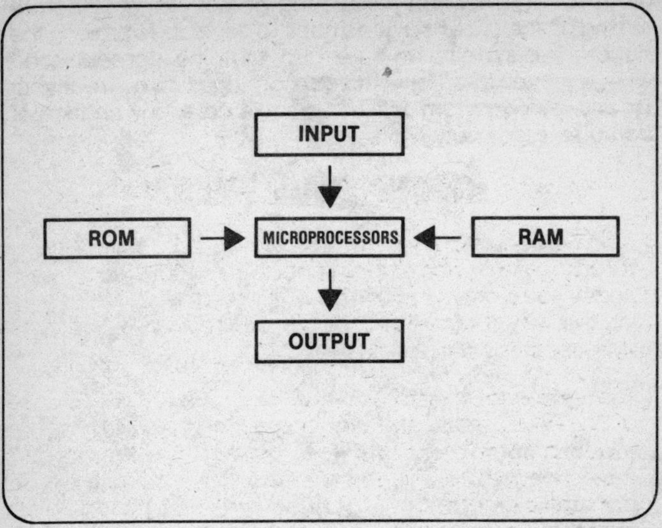

Many television owners wonder whether their sets will be in any way damaged by the game systems. The answer: probably not. The only danger, which manufacturers take great pains to counteract, is that the picture tube will be permanently blemished by phosphor burns left by the games' playfields and scoring displays. Games with pure white in their graphics can damage the screen most easily, but even they take many, many hours of play to do so.

Atari and Activision use no white in their graphics; furthermore, their cartridges automatically change the screen's colors when a game is left on after play ceases, preventing any damage from occurring for hours. When any of the game systems is turned off, the picture tube is relieved of all phosphor memory, so the long burning process must begin all over again the next time the system is used. When left on long enough to cause damage, however, the system causes permanent damage.

You can take preventive measures. First of all, lower the TV's contrast control as much as possible. Second, be sure to turn off your console when not playing games; doing so before turning off the TV set is a good habit to develop. To prolong the life of your system, be sure also that the console is off whenever you insert or withdraw cartridges. If you treat your TV and game system with reasonable care, any chance of damage is very, very slight.

3

NINE STEPS TOWARD MASTERY

Step 1: Reconnaissance

Your first goal in conquering a home video game is to pass the beginner's stage; you will have much less trouble doing so if you read the game's instruction booklet. It is possible to discover independently everything the booklet can tell you, but that time is better spent on learning the subtleties of the game, the parts the booklet does not include. The sooner you learn the basics, therefore, the better.

From one careful reading of the booklet, you will gain a firm command of the three essentials: objectives, controls, and scoring. You will know what you want, learn the rudiments of how to get it, and begin formulating the best and quickest way to get it.

Playing the game before you know the rules can be fun in its own way but it is rarely an effective way to gain true proficiency. Orientation is always the first step.

Step 2: Teamwork

Once you have learned the basics, you need a friend. Game mastery at its best is very much a team effort, and you are about to progress further than many home video players ever do.

You should rely on your friend to take notes during experiments (see Step 7), to supply advice and constructive criticism, and to provide a foil for your own comments and insights. Watching you, he or she will be able to observe the game's workings objectively without the pressure of playing it.

Encourage your friend and share impressions with him. (I use the masculine pronoun for convenience only; women are often excellent video gamers.) When you tell him your ideas, you will both enlighten him and clarify the concepts in your own mind. Teamwork will always help more than it hurts.

Step 3: Concentration

When you are learning a difficult video game, you should not be thinking about what to have for breakfast the next morning. You must learn to channel your attention into the new world you have entered, whether it is outer space, the open sea, or elsewhere.

The off-television excercises discussed in Chapter 7 will train you to devote less mental energy to the mechanics of the game. Once you are comfortable with the controls, you gain the most precious single attribute of an expert: confidence.

Confidence allows you not only to operate the controls without thinking but also to make simple strategic decisions automatically. A MISSILE COMMAND master can know without conscious thought that he has destroyed one enemy missile, although he is already moving on to three more. An intermediate player can never become an expert without confidence, which can, in turn, be reached only through concentration.

Step 4: Psychology

Of the 15 games examined, five can be played in direct competition with another person in which your actions determine his and vice versa. In these games and all others like them, you must analyze not only the intricacies of the program but also those of your opponent's style.

The problem is that he can do the same with you. In any game, the best players consciously vary their styles so as to catch adversaries off guard. You may like a certain tactic in ARMOR BATTLE but, if you use it too often against one opponent, he will begin to expect it, and it will lose its value. For specifics, see the strategies for games such as WARLORDS, ARMOR BATTLE, and SEA BATTLE.

Step 5: Tempo

Even before your first serious attempt at any game, try to get a feeling for its rhythms. (See Chapter 7.) Once you have unconsciously absorbed knowledge of the game's "heartbeat," the inevitable timing and patterns will all begin to fall into place.

Each cartridge's program works in established chronological intervals, which you can learn almost without effort. Once you understand a rhythm, taking advantage of it through synchronization and/or syncopation can be quite simple and will produce fantastic results.

Step 6: Observation

If you see something happen on the screen, remember it. It happened because some detail in the software made it happen; understanding and remembering that detail will certainly help you in the future. You would not, for example, notice casually that the Command Ships in SPACE INVADERS emerge every 16 seconds, but such knowledge, through observation, can certainly come in handy.

The next three chapters contain my own observations and those of other players. You will have to make similar ones for mastery of any other game you choose to learn.

Step 7: Experimentation

Observation is useful because every game is run on a program. Computers work in regular patterns when their programmers do not take the trouble of producing random occurrences, which are rarer than you would think. Given a limited memory capacity, the cartridges can possess only a limited complexity and a limited number of random occurrences.

For the same reason, programs often have tiny bugs, quirks that the programmers either missed or left in deliberately. In either case, the programmers usually consider the flaws insignificant to or unnoticeable by the average player.

The above-average player, however, experiments. He fiddles and fools around with the program until he knows all its ins and outs, finding all irregularities and inadvertent patterns, analyzing all the data he can muster. And whatever he discovers, he puts to good use. The player who knows how to cross the COMBAT screen in the blink of an eye, for instance, has a considerable advantage over any opponent who does not.

Step 8: Memorization

When a game runs on a pattern, it makes sense that you must adopt a complementary pattern for optimum performance. You can accomplish much by familiarity with the mechanics and controls of a game, but, for true virtuosity you need a complete understanding of its inner workings. Therefore, you must memorize.

Whether you have a photographic memory or one like a sieve, you can find a way to remember what is necessary. Your training partner can jot down important numbers or positions while you play, or you can imprint them on your memory while practicing.

Step 9: Practice

Practice is a wonderful thing. All the elements of the game come together at your fingertips while you enjoy all the excitement video games have to offer. Practicing is even better for home video than for the arcade, for each turn costs nothing and has so much to offer. You can perfect your skill at the controls, strengthen your rhythmic sense, confirm and hone your observations, reap the benefits of your experiments, finish any memorization, and have fun all at once. This is the most satisfying of all the steps because you can see your scores grow higher and higher.

Once you have employed these nine steps in the game of your choice, you will find that the accomplishment has placed mastery within your reach without lessening the excitement or the challenge for an instant.

4

ATARI

Most Atari cartridges consist of one basic game program with several optional variations incorporated into the circuits. The different subsidiary "games" included in a cartridge differ only in the variations they feature. Using the GAME SELECT switch on the console, the player can tell the machine which variations he wants by picking the appropriate game number.

The console contains sockets for two controller plugs, one on each side. Two dials, one joystick, or one keyboard can plug into each socket. The joystick control, the most commonly used, also offers a red button that is used differently in different games. The dials, called "paddles" by Atari–a remnant of the old PONG days–spin without stopping in either direction and have different-shaped red buttons. The keyboards must be purchased separately and are used for only four games. One-player games always use the left controller, and the player with the left controller begins every two-player alternating game.

The player can adjust the BLACK-AND-WHITE/COLOR switch to his TV set and the CH 2/CH 3 switch according to the channel that ordinarily gets the weaker reception. Each controller socket has its own difficulty switch (called "skill switches" on the Sears machine made in cooperation with Atari). When the player on the left sets his difficulty switch at **a**, the game usually becomes harder in some way, but for him only.

With the ON/OFF switch at ON and the game number the difficulty level selected, the player can press RESET to begin the game.

ASTEROIDS

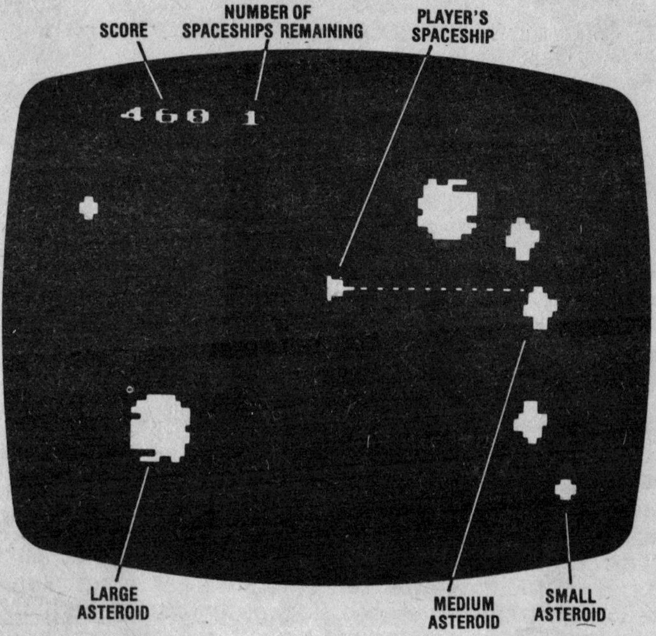

CONTROLS

a. FIRE button

b. Six-directional joystick: THRUST / ROTATE / HYPERSPACE / SHIELD / FLIP

SCORING

a. Large asteroid:	20 points
b. Medium asteroid:	50 points
c. Small asteroid:	100 points
d. Satellite:	200 points

e. UFO: 1,000 points

f. Bonus ship every 5,000, 10,000, or 20,000 points or not at all

DANGERS

a. When the player's ship touches an asteroid, satellite, UFO, or enemy bullet, it is destroyed.
b. When the player runs out of ships, the game ends.

OBSERVATIONS

a. When the player pushes the joystick forward, his ship moves forward, building up speed as it goes. When he releases the joystick, the ship continues, slowing gradually, until the player either lets it glide to a stop or turns it and applies counterthrust.

Turning the joystick to the right or left rotates the ship to the right or left, respectively. If the player wishes to rotate and thrust simultaneously, he can push the joystick diagonally, up and to the left or right.

Pulling the joystick toward him produces the special feature for that game: hyperspace, shield, flip, or none at all. (These features are described later.)

A player pressing FIRE repeatedly can shoot in bursts of two, although he can have more than one burst on the screen at a time. The shots disappear about half a screen's length from the ship, giving the player a limited range, and the player must press the button for every shot he wants to fire. His shots, like the ship itself, can disappear off one edge of the screen and emerge from a predictable spot on the opposite edge.

b. Four large asteroids appear at the beginning of the first screen, with the player's ship facing up in the center. If left alone, the asteroids will float up and down with very slight horizontal movement. An asteroid may cross the screen more than ten times vertically before it does so horizontally.

When a large asteroid is hit, it splits into two medium ones; a medium one, when hit, turns into a small one, and a small one disappears. The ASTEROIDS cartridge offers two types of asteroids, different only in the ways they behave after being hit.

The "slow" asteroids' fragments continue in the same vertical courses as the original large rocks, although they sometimes switch to minutely different diagonals and often increase speed. "Fast" asteroids move no faster, but the fragments break off course at much greater angles. The fast small asteroids, products of two hits, often travel more horizontally than vertically, obviously making survival much harder for the player, and may even move faster.

c. The ASTEROIDS cartridge is equipped with a large memory for an Atari game, capable of handling eight thousand pieces of information at once; still, the programmers were forced to use every available bit. If a player notices that the asteroids flash slightly with more than eight on the screen, it is because the program can show only half of them at a time and so rapidly alternates the two pictures as the next best thing. Furthermore, the player's ship is larger than it appears. It is actually a small black square with tiny, carefully selected areas illuminated to present the silhouette of a ship. The disadvantage of this graphics system is that an asteroid or enemy shot may seem about to miss the player's ship but hit a blackened section of the square instead. The player may then wonder why his ship explodes.

d. When an asteroid collides with the ship, the asteroid splits as though shot, and the player receives the appropriate number of points. The ship is destroyed, of course, and disappears.

The asteroids on the screen maintain their courses while the player's replacement ship is prepared. After at least 2 seconds, it appears facing up at the center of the screen. It sometimes takes longer than that, because two conditions must first be satisfied: there must be no satellite or UFO on the screen and no asteroids within a certain radius of the center. The radius is uncomfortably short, so the replacement ship may appear at a very bad moment, only to be crushed a second later.

The player starts each game with four ships. He may choose–or not choose–to receive ships with every 5,000, 10,000, or 20,000 points.

The instant the player shoots the last asteroid in each screen (necessarily a small one), the next screen appears, not just at the edges but all over the right and left sides of the picture tube. They immediately begin to pursue their vertical courses, with only a narrow central strip temporarily clear. If the player's ship is far from the center when ending one screen, therefore, it may well be demolished within the first second or two of the next.

e. Satellites and UFOs appear only with the player's difficulty switch set at **a**. Both types of enemy craft can shoot "behind" the screen, and both emerge from random points on the screen's left or right edge, never the top or bottom. The game's background rhythm consists of two-beat cycles; either a satellite or a UFO appears after every 19 cycles, give or take one. They are blind to the asteroids, which therefore occasionally collide with enemy shots or the vessels themselves. Although the asteroids then split just as when the player collides with or shoots them, the player receives no points. When a satellite or UFO unexpectedly destroys the last asteroid of a screen, the player may suddenly find himself in a very unpleasant position.

f. A satellite is considerably less formidable than a UFO. I have heard rumors that Atari's programmers nicknamed them "Mr. Bill" and "Mr. Sluggo," respectively. Each satellite is slightly larger than the player's ship and fires two random shots approximately every second. When not destroyed, it usually passes near the player's ship and disappears off the side opposite that from which it emerged. Occasionally, however, a satellite heads straight for the player's ship and destroys it unless the player dodges or does some quick shooting.

Each UFO, on the other hand, is much smaller and fires missiles that travel about twice as fast. The shots are more accurate, moreover, since the UFO fires in a counterclockwise pattern only until it zeroes in on the player's ship; from then on, it usually shoots within about 25° of its target, following the same kind of flight pattern as a satellite.

To make matters worse, a flaw in the program sometimes makes the UFO (not the satellite) invincible. When the player's ship is pointing straight to the left or right and fires at a UFO, its normally lethal shot may pass through the enemy ship without causing any damage. The UFO may then have time to return more deadly fire.

g. Each time the player passes the bonus-ship mark – every 5,000 points, for instance – he hears a series of four high-pitched beeps lasting about 2 seconds. The beeps drown out the sound effect of any satellite or UFO, which in turn drowns out the sound of the player's shots when there is no beeping. Both these sound overlaps work to the player's disadvantage because, under normal circumstances, the player can use his sense of hearing to coordinate his actions. The enemy ships' sound effects serve as warnings, and the average player uses both sight and sound to keep track of his shots.

h. In games with the HYPERSPACE feature, the player's ship disappears the instant he pulls back on the joystick. It reappears about one second later in a randomly chosen location. He can use hyperspace as many times per game as he pleases.

The feature is useful mainly for escaping rocks that the player cannot shoot before colliding with them; the ship accelerates so slowly that thrusting is often futile. Although it thus saves the ship from certain destruction, hyperspace still has its risks because of the random nature of the ship's rematerialization. The more asteroids remain on the screen when the ship vanishes, the greater the chances that it will reappear directly in the path of a hurtling asteroid–or even in the middle of one – and be destroyed instantly.

i. When the player has SHIELD at his disposal, he can make any threatening asteroids, shots, or enemy craft pass through him harmlessly. When he pulls back the joystick, the ship is surrounded by shields that permit any object to pass through it without damage to either.

One catch is that the ship can neither move nor fire when behind its shield. Another drawback, even more serious, is that the ship explodes when the shield is held for more than

2 seconds. The player cannot expect to be able to survive a collision with a large asteroid: 2 seconds of the way through the asteroid, he would be forced either to release the shield and be destroyed or to keep it on and explode.

Even after he releases the joystick and the shield disappears, he must wait about a second before he can use the shield again safely.

j. The FLIP feature enables the player to rotate his ship 180° in the blink of an eye. The device does save time in maneuvering, but targets are often not exactly behind the ship, so some slight adjustment after FLIP may still be required for perfect aim. Furthermore, flipping offers no protection against satellite and UFO bullets, so its usefulness is limited.

k. The game's difficulty increases in relation to the number of large asteroids beginning successive screens. The first screen begins with only four large asteroids; the second and several thereafter, with six; and those from about 15,000 points on, with eight. Since each large asteroid ultimately splits into two medium or small ones, no more than 16 asteroids will ever be on the screen at a time.

The first satellite appears at about 1,000 points; the first UFO, at about 8,000. After the first UFO, only one or two satellites appear for the game's duration.

l. No matter how many points the player earns, the score display can show only five figures. He "turns the game over" every 100,000 points, sending it back to 0. He must therefore keep track of high scores by himself, remembering how many hundreds of thousands of points he has scored.

m. The player can choose fast or slow asteroids, bonus ship level, special features, and singles or doubles. In doubles, one player plays until he loses his first ship; the other then takes over and does the same, after which the first player resumes with his second ship, and so forth, until both players' games have ended.

There is also a simpler version of the game for one or two young children. In Atari's recent international ASTEROIDS tournament, all contestants were required to play with fast asteroids, hyperspace, and bonus ships every 20,000 points.

n. In Chapter 11, I contrast in detail the ASTEROIDS cartridge and its arcade counterpart. The home version is somewhat harder in general, because the player's ship reacts more slowly to the controls, especially the thrust. There is also much less room in which to maneuver freely, since the ship and asteroids are all considerably larger in relation to the screen. On the other hand, the maximum number of large asteroids starting a screen is smaller than in the arcade game.

Atari also produces ASTEROIDS software for its 400 and 800 home computers. The program has unimpressive graphics and sound effects, but screens can start with as many as 18 asteroids, even more than in the arcade version. For an added touch, from one to four players can control ships on the screen at once, each player with his own score.

STRATEGIES

a. First learn to maneuver and aim your ship. The young children's version is actually useful for learning the tricks of maneuvering: how to start, stop, turn, and so on. Once you are comfortable with steering, you can train in a faster game—but still with slow asteroids—to perfect your shooting. Then push the difficulty switch to **a** so that you can learn the habits of satellites and UFOs. Mastering the mechanics of ASTEROIDS is half the game.

b. No matter what variations you have chosen, it is wise to stay in the center of the screen as much as possible, turning to eliminate asteroids rather than chasing them. When you can rotate a stationary ship, your aim is more accurate.

c. Moreover, the farther you are from the edges, the less chance you have of being surprised by an asteroid or enemy craft. There are rarely as many as 16 asteroids on the screen at a time, so it should not be too difficult to keep track of them all. You must learn the "wrap-around" angles, enabling yourself to predict where and in which direction any asteroid going off the edge will appear.

When you develop at least a basic idea of each rock's trajectory, you will know which ones pose the greatest threat to you at the moment. You should try to shoot the ones that threaten to come near to you soonest. Since you stay in the center most of the time, you will soon be able to recognize the most obviously menacing trajectories.

The slow asteroids' courses are extremely easy to plot because they always travel more or less vertically. Simply shoot the asteroids nearest you and you will theoretically never be hit by one.

The fast rocks are much more interesting to evade, and they give ASTEROIDS its challenge. Facing threats from all directions is what makes the arcade version so popular, and you should switch to fast asteroids as soon as you have gained enough confidence.

d. The small asteroids, faster and harder targets, can be the most threatening. Treat them, therefore, as primary targets.

e. When shooting a medium-sized asteroid, fire twice in a row, hoping to score two hits and destroy the rock completely. If you miss the small rock, watch where it goes. Small asteroids are so dangerous that some players prefer to shoot only nearby mediums to be sure they don't miss on the second shot and create small rocks.

f. As for large rocks, don't let them come too close if they are heading toward you. If you do, it is better to maneuver or hyperspace out of the way than to try shooting the asteroid, producing dangerous fragments. Large asteroids are more dangerous if you are using SHIELD rather than HYPERSPACE, so eliminate them early each screen in games with SHIELD. With hyperspace at your disposal, there is no strong reason not to shoot them early, but you do create two asteroids for each one you hit, cluttering the screen unnecessarily.

g. Shoot the last asteroid or two of each screen from the center. If you are near the left or right side when the last one is destroyed, you will probably be crushed instantly by the next screen.

h. If you realize that you are about to crash, get as many points from it as possible. Try to shoot or ram an enemy vessel rather than be hit by an asteroid. After a ship has been destroyed, you must watch the center of the screen to be ready for the next one's materialization. Players who do not stay prepared during this crucial time often lose their new ships without firing a shot, whereas more alert and experienced players can use shield or hyperspace or at least fire, getting the new ship off to a healthy start.

i. SHIELD is the most advantageous feature for most players; HYPERSPACE, the next; and FLIP, the least.

To use your shield well, you must never use it too long, and you must keep the intervals between uses at safe lengths. To accomplish all this, you should learn exactly the right moment to shield yourself against an asteroid. If you do it too soon, you may need the shield too long and explode; if you do it too late, the asteroid may reach you first. Do not use the shield at all with large asteroids unless you manage to shoot them first, making their size more manageable.

j. With hyperspace, too, you must be quick. Not every player reacts in time to an emergency, and alertness is essential. You should use hyperspace only in emergencies, of course, since there is always some risk of rematerializing in the wrong place. The more asteroids on the screen, the more worried you should be about hyperspace, but it is never completely safe. When you must use it, you need peripheral vision to see instantly where you reappear. If you are in the path of an asteroid or enemy vessel, you can immediately decide either to shoot your way out or to use hyperspace again provided you are lucky enough to have time.

k. If you choose FLIP, you can learn its usefulness with some practice. No matter how proficient you become, though, it will never be more than an offensive device. FLIP saves no time if you are pointing 90° away from your target, and it will never protect you if you miss. All in all, it is slightly better than nothing.

l. When you hear the beeps of a bonus ship, look out for satellites or UFOs that may suddenly jeopardize the ship you currently control. You can't hear the sounds of their engines, so you have to watch the screen's borders carefully, another example of the need for good peripheral vision.

m. Shoot satellites and UFOs by predicting their courses, aiming slightly ahead of them, and firing repeatedly. If they get by the first time, repeat the procedure until you succeed. UFOs which appear directly to your right or left are the most dangerous, because your shots sometimes pass right through them; it is therefore a good idea to slide up or down a little before turning and shooting. Watch your enemy's shots as well so that your hyperspace or shield can save you.

n. Beginners occasionally panic when trapped between two fast-approaching asteroids. Experienced players are confident enough, however, to turn and shoot one rock, then use HYPERSPACE or SHIELD to escape the other.

o. Don't let apparent "near misses" fool you. Even if an asteroid or enemy shot seems about to skim past your port or starboard bow, it may still hit the black part of the square, which is really your ship. (See Observation c.)

p. The interval between shooting the two last rocks in each screen is often the longest, since there is no longer any choice of targets. UFOs thus have ample chance to appear, and they are at their most dangerous with no obstructions between them and the ship.

If a UFO emerges at such a time from the side of the screen your ship is facing, you will almost always have time to turn and shoot it before it homes in on you. Since you are in the center of the screen (Strategy g), you must develop some degree of accuracy.

If the UFO appears behind you, however, you are taking more of a risk if you rotate to shoot back. The closer the UFO comes, the more dangerous its shots. Instead of taking the precious time to turn, you may prefer to go into hyperspace, confusing your enemy for long enough to draw a bead on it. There is still some chance of rematerializing too close to it, though, or in the asteroid's path, so not even this method is perfect.

There is yet another choice. If you can shoot the asteroid quickly, do so. The UFO will almost surely perish soon in the midst of the new screen.

q. The tactic of "hunting," extremely successful in arcade ASTEROIDS (See Chapter 11), does not work in the home version. The ship does not react quite sensitively enough to the controls, for one thing, but the chief danger is that the UFO will collide with or shoot the last asteroid. When the new screen comes on, you will probably be destroyed, since hunting from the center is ineffective. Because it does not permit hunting and has less responsive controls, the home game can be useful in mastering the arcade version, just as some runners do some of their training with weights on their legs. The cartridge, though, does provide more than enough excitement in itself.

GAME VARIATIONS

GAME NO.	SPEED	EXTRA LIFE	FEATURES	GAME NO.
1	S	5	H	34
2	F	5	H	35
3	S	10	H	36
4	F	10	H	37
5	S	20	H	38
6	F	20	H	39
7	S	N	H	40
8	F	N	H	41
9	S	5	SH	42
10	F	5	SH	43
11	S	10	SH	44
12	F	10	SH	45
13	S	20	SH	46
14	F	20	SH	47
15	S	N	SH	48
16	F	N	SH	49
17	S	5	FL	50
18	F	5	FL	51
19	S	10	FL	52
20	F	10	FL	53
21	S	20	FL	54
22	F	20	FL	55
23	S	N	FL	56
24	F	N	FL	57
25	S	5	W	58
26	F	5	W	59
27	S	10	W	60
28	F	10	W	61
29	S	20	W	62
30	F	20	W	63
31	S	N	W	64
32	F	N	W	65
33	CHILDREN			66

ONE PLAYER

TWO PLAYERS

LEGEND

SPEED:
S = Slow
F = Fast

FEATURES:
H = Hyperspace
SH = Shield
FL = Flip
W = Without Features

EXTRA LIFE:
5 = 1 Extra ship every 5,000 points
10 = 1 Extra ship every 10,000 points
20 = 1 Extra ship every 20,000 points
N = No extra ships

COMBAT

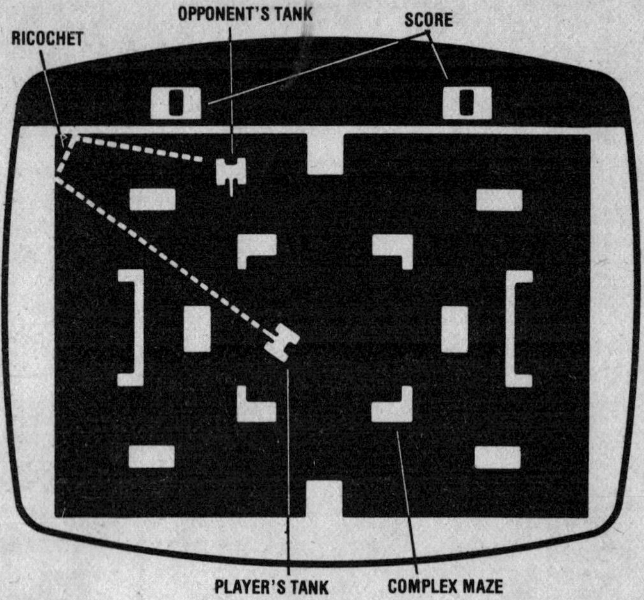

TANK-PONG

CONTROLS

a. Joystick controlling speed, rotation, and/or thrust.
b. FIRE button.

SCORING

a. The player scores one point for each hit on his opponent.

DANGERS

a. The player's opponent does his best to shoot the player's tank, biplane, or jet.

OBSERVATIONS

a. Each game lasts exactly 2 minutes and 16 seconds. The players may agree beforehand to compete either for a fixed number of points or for the lead when the time runs out.

b. With 27 different games, the COMBAT cartridge offers the players many variations, including choice of weapons: tanks, biplanes, or jets. In any case, each player controls at least one, causing it to maneuver and shoot aggressively and defensively. The tanks and jets are viewed from above and the biplanes from the side, but all three types of conflict share many characteristics; after all, they run on the same program.

Each player can rotate his tank or plane, for instance, to any one of 16 positions. The planes are always moving forward with speeds controlled by the players, but the tanks can only roll forward or stand still, never accelerate. For convenience sake, I will call the left player's weapon the left tank, left biplane, or left jet and follow the same practice with the right player's weapon.

c. Acceleration is to the planes what thrust is to the tanks, and planes and tanks alike can be rotated. The joystick works differently in each case, though, as outlined below:

1. Each tank maneuvers like the player's ship in ASTEROIDS. Pushing the joystick forward rolls the tank forward, pushing to the left or right rotates the tank to the left or right, and pulling back has no effect.

2. Pushing the joystick to the left or right slows or accelerates the player's biplane. Pushing forward makes the biplane appear to dive, actually turn right; pulling back makes it seem to climb, actually turn left. Because the biplanes can fly upside down or at any other angle, "climb" and "dive" are misleading terms. Like tanks and jets, they simply turn left or right. The confusion is brought about by the player's profile view: the biplanes should be thought of as abstract objects, faster than tanks but slower than jets.

3. Pushing the joystick to the left or right rotates the player's jet to the left or right. Pushing forward accelerates it, and pulling back decelerates it.

The joystick can move in eight directions, not four. Pushing it up and to the left, for example, turns the tank forward and to the left, slows the biplane and turns it to the right, or accelerates the jet and turns it to the left.

d. Depending on the game number, pressing the FIRE button can cause several different events. The player's tank or plane can fire guided missiles; after the player shoots, he can use the joystick to turn the missile slightly to the left or right. Beginners may not realize that such an action simultaneously rotates the player's tank or plane.

The players can also choose games with regular missiles, ones that travel in straight paths at all times. The planes' missiles can always disappear off one edge of the screen and emerge from the opposite side, continuing until reaching the end of their range. The tank screen is always enclosed, however, so that missiles detonate whenever they reach the screen's edge.

In the version of COMBAT known as Tank-Pong, the tank's missiles actually rebound off the walls and barriers. The players can choose beforehand whether the tanks can be hit by direct shots and ricochets or only by ricochets.

In almost every missile variation, each player can have only one shot on the screen at a time, that is, he must wait for each shot to detonate by hitting an enemy, a wall, or the end of its range before he can shoot the next. (If he wishes, he can fire again without lifting his finger from the button, shooting each missile automatically the instant the last has detonated.) The one exception to the rule occurs in certain biplane games in which the biplanes fire not missiles but machine guns. The program produces that effect by allowing each player to have not one but eight bullets out at a time. Their range is much shorter, though, only about the length of three planes, so keeping the FIRE button down produces many bullets per second; the target must be much closer, though. A player with his difficult switch set at **a** fires missiles with only about two-thirds the normal range.

e. Because every battle uses the same program, there exist certain universal similarities. Whenever one player's weapon is hit, for instance, the force of impact carries it an inch or two, also spinning it rapidly counterclockwise. When the tank or plane finally recovers, it is **always** facing three positions, or 67.5° to the left of where it was facing when hit. If it had a missile out, that missile instantly disappears.

The victorious tank or plane is automatically rotated one position, or 22.5° to the left. Once the victim stops spinning, both players regain control simultaneously. A victorious plane has meanwhile continued to move forward, carrying it past its helplessly whirling opponent. The program is designed so that each point can begin with the players on an equal footing, but it achieves that effect only in the air battles.

f. If one tank is near a wall or barrier and is hit from the other side, the force of the shot can carry it through the wall or barrier. If that wall is an outside wall, the victim tank disappears and emerges from the opposite edge of the screen. The tank always stops on one side of walls or the other, never in the walls themselves.

Apart from being hit, there is only one way to cross "behind" the screen, and that one is little known. The player must drive to one of the four corners of the screen, then maneuver into the following position: touching both walls and facing the right wall (the right wall from the perspective of the corner; in the bottom left corner, for instance, the bottom wall). The position can be reached quickly with practice. When the player then moves the tank forward, it "wraps around" to the opposite corner. I don't know why, but the same technique works with interior barriers with concave right angles. If the player wishes, he can shift his tank from the inside of the barrier to the outside in the blink of an eye.

g. There are no barriers in the open-field variations of Tank, just the four outside walls. The easy maze, though, presents six well-placed obstructions, and the complex maze offers fourteen. It is sometimes possible for the left or right tank to shoot through the tip of a barrier's corner.

h. Tank-Pong is a fascinating variation. The player's missile keeps bouncing off walls in predictable patterns until it either hits the enemy or reaches the end of its range. Here is a list of minor observations concerning Tank-Pong:

1. When it rebounds, the missile emits a beep that rises on the scale with each bounce.

2. The missile bounces with geometric logic except when it is fired at a perpendicular wall; instead of bouncing straight back as it should, it is deflected about 30° to the right.

3. In no variation of Tank-Pong can a tank be hit by its own missile. The missile passes through it without damage.

4. In the Tank-Pong games with no direct hits possible, each missile possesses greater range. The player therefore has more chance of success with each shot, but he can fire fewer shots in 2 minutes and 16 seconds.

   If the enemy tank is next to a wall in a game without direct hits, the player's missile may pass through the enemy the first time and then hit him on the rebound.

5. The player may find his missile bouncing off several walls and stopping just short of the target. It will not work simply to advance straight toward the site of the first rebound and shoot again. For some reason, the missile will make the same bounces and disappear in the same spot as the first time, just short of the target.

i. The program's irregularities reach their most bizarre in the Tank-Pong games. One important example occurs in Game 9 (easy maze, no direct hits). The left tank can destroy the right tank in 15 different ways without even leaving its starting place simply by rotating and shooting. Ironically, the one direction in which firing will not destroy the right tank is straight toward it.

The right tank can accomplish the same feat by firing in any of ten directions, including the two closest to its starting position. The difference between the left and right tanks' abilities here is due to tiny asymmetries in the maze.

Just for fun, see what happens when the right tank immediately turns and fires at the far right wall, before its enemy can move. Now repeat the same experiment with the left tank.

j. In the variation known as Invisible Tank, each tank is invisible except when hit, firing, or running into a wall. Since each player is rarely aware of both tanks' precise positions, this variation introduces a greater element of luck.

k. In every tank battle, visible or invisible, rebound or direct, the two tanks start facing each other on opposite sides of the screen, out of each other's range. A sneaky player, however, can still shoot and score.

The RESET switch begins the game when it is depressed **and** released. When held down, however, it permits the player to shoot harmless missiles, ones with unlimited range. If two players are starting a game with an open field, for instance, and one holds RESET down and fires, his missile will cross the screen again and again, passing through walls and tanks without stopping. Neither tank can move.

An imaginative player will hold RESET down and fire, then release when his missile is about to hit the enemy. The missile suddenly stops being harmless and hits his opponent's tank. The technique works for every tank battle except those with no direct hits. It is not part of the game, of course, but it can be done once or twice just as a joke before starting to play seriously.

l. The players can choose air battles with or without clouds. The clouds are two large white patches on the screen behind which the planes can turn, hide, shoot, or be shot.

m. Biplanes and jets can both change speed and direction and can "wrap around" the screen whenever their pilots wish. The main differences are that jets are faster and have slightly longer-range missiles.

n. With practice, the player can pilot his plane into a narrow, invisible zone between the top and bottom of the screen. Hiding just above the top, he can fly horizontally with only his landing gear (biplane) or wing tip (jet) showing. With such a small target, his opponent will find it very difficult to score any points.

o. The players can choose to play with two biplanes or jets each. One player's pair of jets, set close together, respond identically to his controls, producing a double-image effect. The players need less accurate aim, and points are scored more quickly because each shot sends twice as many missiles after twice as many targets.

p. The left player can pilot one jet against the right player's three. The match is still even: although the right player can rake the sky with three missiles at once, the left player has three different targets. He has the disadvantage in the biplane counterpart, however: his one ungainly bomber presents almost as easy a target as the right player's three biplanes combined, and it can fire only one missile at a time, compared to their three.

STRATEGIES

a. Do everything in your power to know the COMBAT controls, handling, and steering better than your opponent. If both of you know the game inside out, you will need all the skill and strategy you have.

b. Know your opponent's tactics and style better than

1. he thinks you do
2. he knows yours

Being able to predict his next move will win you many, many points.

c. It is not wise to keep the FIRE button down at all times. You will keep firing automatically, depriving yourself of the opportunity to time shots correctly.

d. Since the action is so fast, almost every accurate shot in the air battles is fired at close range. You will therefore actually do better if you set your difficulty switch at **a**. You will not mind having shorter shots, and you will be able to fit more shots into each game.

e. The guided missiles constitute by far the most important element of any game that features them, so much so that they render much strategy and planning unnecessary. Once you have perfected your missile-guiding skills, not many opponents can offer you much of a challenge. Simply advance toward the enemy between two of his sixteen lines of fire; once you are in range, chances are that you will score the first hit. Keep pursuing, shooting him again and again, until you reach the center of the screen, from which no skillful player can be driven. The position is overwhelmingly advantageous in any open field or easy maze.

You cannot hold the center of the screen in air battles, of course, but you will still win if you guide missiles better than your opponent.

f. It is also very useful to be able to anticipate your position after being hit. Just remember the direction you were facing when hit and think three-sixteenths to the left. You will then know in which direction you must turn to face your opponent and if you must turn at all, and you can set your controls accordingly beforehand. If you deduce that you will be facing your opponent already, you can dazzle him by pressing FIRE in advance, scoring a hit the instant you come out of your spin. Making the greatest possible preparations always helps to even the odds after a hit.

When you hit your opponent be sure to pursue your advantage. He is usually carried farther in the same direction, so all you need to do is recover your previous aim. That means turning just one position clockwise, compensating for the automatic counterclockwise shift a moment before. (See Observation e.) You can often score at least one more hit in that manner.

Sometimes, however, your opponent is carried behind the screen by your shot and reappears behind you. He may have the advantage now, but you should start rotating to the left to face him as soon as possible.

g. When both players have enough experience, Tank with mazes can require a great deal of strategy. You and your opponent will often reach apparent standoffs, each on one side of a barrier corner, threatening to shoot the other if he advances an inch. Neither of you has a target, but neither of you can advance enough to find one.

In such a situation, you might want to turn a bit away from the wall, making him think you're going to try for another angle. When he rushes around the corner for the kill, turn quickly back and blast him.

Catching your opponent by surprise is all-important. If you see him fire from behind the corner, ask yourself when he will be able to fire his next shot. If his difficulty switch is set at **b** and there is no wall or barrier for his last missile to detonate against, you probably have time to advance a fraction of an inch, turn toward him, and fire before he can shoot again. You will have benefited from his mistake; remember that there is never any reason to fire when you know your shot will miss.

h. If your enemy's tank is behind you and you know you cannot escape being hit, try at least to station your tank so that the shot will knock it through a wall or barrier, giving you ample time for recovery afterward.

i. You can often use the special short cut described in Observation f to escape a pursuing tank and even to turn the tables on your adversary. You must practice the maneuver alone, though, to be sure that you can always accomplish it without difficulty or delay in battle.

j. If you experiment enough by yourself in Tank-Pong and keep in your head a catalogue of promising shots from just five key locations, you will be just about unbeatable. Not even an opponent who knows the ricochet patterns well will be able to match your accuracy.

If you are in unfamiliar territory, however, there are still certain tactics you can use to keep your opponent spinning and to stay out of trouble yourself. You must learn to recognize at least the simple one- and two-bounce shots, using your knowledge either to hit your opponent once you realize he is in your line of fire or to set traps for him to advance into. Likewise, you must always watch the enemy tank and keep track of at least its missiles' approximate potential trajectories. You can thereby avoid walking into ambushes and accidental pitfalls.

There is always some luck involved, but it never hurts to line one shot up while keeping an eye on your last. You need peripheral vision, obviously, for you must also check periodically on your opponent and his missiles. If you see your shot fall just short of his tank, remember that simply advancing and trying the same shot again will do you no good (as set forth in Observation h).

In Game 9, you can gain the initiative and the first point by turning just one position to the left or right and firing. Remember that you must act quickly, before an experienced opponent can do the same thing first. Once you have scored the first hit, he will be so disoriented that you can follow up with several more just by rotating to the appropriate position and firing.

If your adversary does manage to shoot first in Game 9, you will still have time to escape if you know the path his missile is bound to follow.

k. You must know Tank to do well at Invisible Tank. Since you cannot see even your own tank most of the time, you must know purely from sound how far you have traveled since your last sighting and in which direction. Practice hard to recognize how much you have turned, for rotation affects both maneuvering and aim.

Try not to run into walls, because that gives your position away. When your opponent does see you, turn and move away before he can trace you. Watch for him as well; try to follow him and get him in your sights. Since you do not want him to know your location, you will fire only with good chances of success, so neither of you will score many points.

There is still much skill involved in winning the game. Invisible Tank-Pong, on the other hand, involves mainly luck; each hit scored usually comes as a surprise to both players.

l. When fighting with planes, know the "wrap-around" angles for both planes and missiles. The screen is like an infinitely long vertical and horizontal scroll; if you fail to treat it as such, you are in for trouble.

Use the clouds, if you have chosen them, to trick your opponent by turning sharply or changing speed. If you are biplane pilots with machine guns, keep FIRE down at all times: the three plane's-lengths ahead of you will always be deadly. The only two times you do not want your machine gun firing are these:

1. You are about to emerge from an edge of the screen near your opponent, and you don't want him to know it until it is too late for him to escape.

2. You plan to ambush him from a cloud by turning suddenly. If you fire early, he will instinctively turn away.

m. Do whatever you can to stay just behind the enemy plane. If the two of you are flying abreast, slow down until you can get behind him and start shooting. If you find yourself just ahead of him, however, watch to see where he shoots and swerve quickly to avoid his line of fire before he can shoot again. With proper planning, you should be after him once more within 2 seconds.

n. Whether you are using tanks or planes, you should both agree in advance whether you are playing up to a certain number of points or until the end of the game. The latter is customary, and you can take advantage of it.

If you manage to accumulate a substantial lead in the first part of the game and winning is important to you, you can easily stall the action, denying your opponent even a chance of catching up with you. In Tank, it is never difficult to create a standoff in any of the mazes, although the open field is a problem. In Invisible Tank, you can stay quietly hidden for as long as you like.

If you practice the maneuver enough, you can hide your plane as described in Observation n, making it very difficult to hit, especially since you can easily accelerate or decelerate to dodge the few threatening shots your opponent can muster. Do not shoot back at him if you wish to stay hidden: if you hit him, your own plane will immediately pop out of its hiding place. If your adversary is winning and you see him attempting to hide, you must shoot him before he achieves his goal. The more he has practiced, the less chance you have of hitting him in time.

GAME VARIATIONS

	GAME NO.	GUIDED MISSILE	MACHINE GUNS	DIRECT HIT	BILLIARD HIT	OPEN FIELD	EASY MAZE	COMPLEX MAZE	CLOUDS
TANK	1	X				X			
	2	X					X		
	3						X		
	4	X						X	
	5							X	
TANK-PONG	6			X	X		X		
	7			X	X			X	
	8				X	X			
	9				X		X		
INVISIBLE TANK	10	X				X			
	11	X					X		
INVISIBLE TANK-PONG	12			X	X		X		
	13				X	X			
	14				X		X		
BIPLANE	15	X							X
	16								X
	17		X						X
	18		X			X			
2 vs. 2	19	X				X			
1 vs. 3	20					X			
JET FIGHTER	21	X							X
	22								X
	23	X				X			
	24					X			
2 vs. 2	25	X							X
1 vs. 3	26	X				X			
2 vs. 2	27					X			

These are mean ways of winning, of course, and frustrating ways of losing. They do add another dimension to the game, though, and they make good performance during the early points especially important. Use them only if you know your opponent would do the same to you.

MISSILE COMMAND

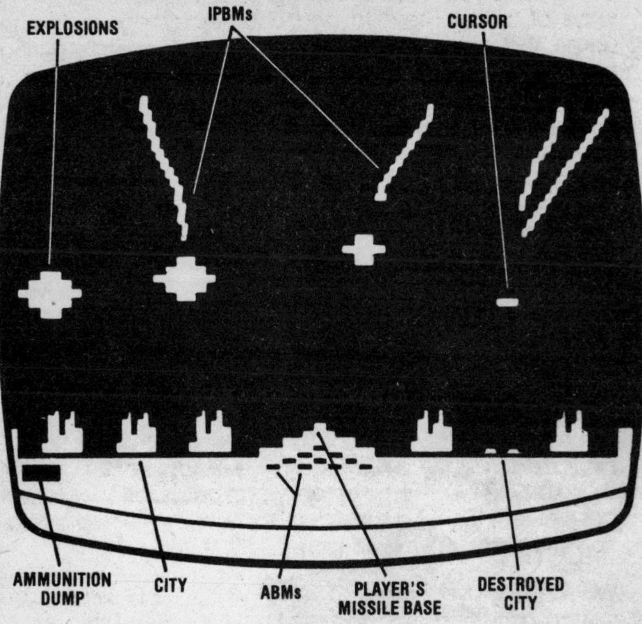

CONTROLS

a. Eight-directional joystick

b. FIRE button

SCORING

a. IPBM: 25–150 points

b. Smart missile: 125–750 points

c. Bonus at the end of each wave

d. Extra city every 10,000 points

DANGERS

a. When any enemy missile hits a city or the missile base, the site is destroyed.

b. The player cannot begin any wave without cities, so the game ends once he has run out of them.

OBSERVATIONS

a. Evil Krytolians are attacking the planet Zardon, and you are responsible for protecting six cities on the planet's surface. The aliens' interplanetary ballistic missiles (IPBMs) descend swiftly from the sky, but you have antiballistic missiles (ABMs) with which to intercept them. How long can you withstand the Krytolian attack?

b. The player's supply of 30 ABMs is replenished at the beginning of each wave, distributed in three blocks of ten. Two of these blocks begin in a subterranean ammunition dump at bottom left; the third set of ten appears in pyramid formation in the player's missile base.

When the player wishes to fire a missile, he presses a red button, and the shot is released from the missile base. ABMs always travel at the same speed; the farther away a missile's target, the longer the ABM takes to detonate. (See next observation.)

If the white dot at the summit of the missile base is hit by any enemy missile, all the base's missiles are destroyed. A replacement block of ten is automatically brought up from the ammo dump, so the player can fire again in a very short time. When he uses up a block of ten by shooting, he also receives an immediate replacement from underground provided he has not already shot or lost all 30 ABMs in that wave.

c. The player controls a cursor, or target marker, that can move in any of eight directions. Whenever he presses FIRE, an ABM is launched toward the cursor; even if he then moves the cursor away, the ABM will detonate when it reaches the point the cursor occupied during the launching.

The cursor can usually be maneuvered with greater accuracy vertically or horizontally than diagonally and with greater ease in one direction than in a mixture of two. The player can be surer of his aim, for instance, when shifting straight to the left than when moving to the left and up a bit.

The player can choose a fast or slow cursor. Both types have advantages: the fast one can reach a desired target site more quickly, but the slow one needs less precision to get it to stop at exactly the right spot. Even the slow cursor, though, speeds up as the game progresses.

d. The player can have no more than three ABMs on the screen at a time. If he tries to launch a fourth, a beeping sound will indicate that he must wait for one of the three already on the screen to detonate and die out before he can fire again.

e. When the difficulty switch is set at **a**, all the ABMs move more slowly. Not only must the player aim sooner to produce each explosion, but also he can launch fewer missiles in, say, a 15-second period.

f. At the end of each wave, the player is awarded 5–30 points for each ABM he has left and 100–600 for each city. Before the next wave begins, the bonus city he may have earned appears in one of the six urban sites. If he already has six cities on the screen, however, his extras are held for him until the next wave or whenever he has empty sites. Until he runs out of bonus cities, therefore, he will have six cities on the screen at the beginning of every wave.

g. IPBMs descend slowly from the top of the screen in the first wave, sometimes straight down but usually at a slight angle. If left alone, each IPBM will fall without changing its course until it strikes the surface of Zardon, when it detonates. If it lands on open ground or on a previously demolished city, it explodes without effect. When it hits a standing city or the top of the missile base, however, the whole sky flashes, and the city or base is destroyed.

Not all IPBMs which land are deadly, and most are intercepted before they land. Each of the players' ABMs, upon reaching its detonation site, produces a wide nuclear cloud that lasts for about a second before shrinking back to nothingness. Any IPBM whose white tip touches such a nuclear cloud detonates early, never reaching the ground. Sometimes, in fact, one IPBM will run into the nuclear cloud caused by the destruction of another, so both of them are taken care of.

h. The Krytolians' most diabolical armament is not the IPBM but the cruise missile. The player, when selecting his game, can choose between smart and dumb cruise missiles; both varieties are more dangerous than IPBMs.

Dumb cruise missiles appear at the top of the screen and fall quickly to the ground, always directly toward standing cities or the top of the missile base. They do not change course if their targets are destroyed, in which case they produce the same small mushroom clouds as IPBMs. Luckily, dumb cruise missiles can be destroyed with ABMs almost as easily as IPBMs can.

Smart cruise missiles, however, are much trickier. Each one can sense if there is an explosion in front of it; if there is, it knows enough to stop in midair until the threatening nuclear cloud has vanished. If it has to, the smart cruise missile will even back up to avoid a spreading nuclear cloud. It retreats in its own path, not necessarily straight up, and waits until the cloud disperses enough for it to proceed. To destroy a smart cruise missile with one shot, therefore, requires considerable accuracy, since the enemy must be on or very near the detonation site at the instant the ABM explodes.

i. There can be only two groups of enemy missiles on the screen at a time, each group consisting of either one to four IPBMs or one cruise missile.

A cruise missile may head for either a city or a missile base. It is interesting that a group of IPBMs can be aimed only at cities or at the missile base. If one IPBM is set to fall on a city, the others in the group will either land on cities or narrowly miss the missile base; if one is aimed at the missile base, the others will all miss cities narrowly. When the player exterminates one group or it lands, the next group appears unless the wave is nearly over.

j. All the point values are at their lowest in Waves 1 and 2, doubled in Waves 3 and 4, tripled in Waves 5 and 6, quadrupled in Waves 7 and 8, quintupled in Waves 9 and 10, and sextupled from Wave 11 on. The only catch is that play becomes much harder, with enemy missiles quicker and more numerous. The screen's colors change, too, as a signal to the player. The following table shows how the game reaches its greatest difficulty in Wave 13:

Wave	Enemy Missiles	Colors
1	12 IPBMs	
2	14 IPBMs	Black sky, brown ground
3	16 IPBMs	
4	14 IPBMs	Black sky, green ground
5	14 IPBMs	
6	14 IPBMs, 1 cruise missile	Black sky, blue ground
7	16 IPBMs, 2 cruise missiles	
8	16 IPBMs, 2 cruise missiles	Black sky, red ground
9	18 IPBMs, 3 cruise missiles	
10	16 IPBMs, 3 cruise missiles	Green sky, blue ground
11	[illegible] ruise missiles	
12	[illegible] se missiles	Green sky, black ground
13	[illegible] es	Blue sky, green ground
14 o[illegible]	[illegible] ssiles	

The en[illegible] every other wave up to Wav[illegible] continue to appear every other wave until Wave 25, when the color cycle starts over from the beginning. The game never becomes easier after Wave 13, however.

k. The score display can hold only six digits, so the game "turns over" whenever the player scores 1,000,000 points. That process takes so long, however, that it is not hard to keep track of the millions scored.

l. Instead of beginning his game with Wave 1, the player can handicap himself by starting as high as Wave 7, Wave 11, or Wave 15. After a few minutes of play, of course, the difference disappears; the player has simply chosen to forego the easier waves. There is also a version on the cartridge especially for young children in which the action is slower than in Wave 1. The children's game and all the others can be played either alone or by two alternating players.

m. Atari's original arcade MISSILE COMMAND is also a very good game. These are its principal differences from the home version:

1. The action is in general somewhat faster.

2. The player controls three missile bases, not one. Alpha Base is on the far left, Omega Base is on the far right, and Delta Base is in the center. Each base, with its own FIRE button, can launch up to ten ABMs per wave.

3. The player can have as many as eight missiles on the screen at a time, not three.

4. The cursor is controlled not by a joystick but by an Atari Trak-Ball, a much more sensitive control.

5. IPBMs fall not in groups but separately. An IPBM may also split into two missiles, which then head for different cities or missile bases.

6. The enemy possesses bombers and killer satellites that cross the screen one at a time and drop more IPBMs, even splintering ones, until they either vanish off the opposite edge or are destroyed.

7. Fortunately, the player can lose no more than three cities in a single wave.

n. Atari has also created a MISSILE COMMAND program for its home computer. The game is similar to the arcade version in every way except that the player uses only one missile base and an underground ammunition dump, as in the home video cartridge.

STRATEGIES

a. Learn the game using a slow cursor and dumb cruise missiles or even in the children's version. Once you have gained enough confidence, take on the smart cruise missiles. Only with faultless control can you then handle the fast cursor; it is usually wiser to stick to the slow one, as most players do, so that you can devote less attention to maneuvering and more to strategy.

b .Watch all enemy missiles carefully, observing in which direction they are falling and how fast. Once you perceive precisely the destination of one IPBM out of a group, you can deduce where all the others are headed and whether you need to worry about them.

c .You must learn to ignore every ABM you fire; if you watch to see it detonate you will miss other precious opportunities to aim and fire. You can watch out of the corner of your eye to see if it intercepts the enemy missile or not, but you should soon have enough experience to judge your accuracy as soon as you fire.

d .When possible, move your cursor in only one direction between shots. You will then be able to aim and fire more quickly and easily than if you were to shift it twice every time to get it just right.

e .You should be aware of when you already have three ABMs on the screen, so that you will not try to launch another in a desperate situation and get an unpleasant surprise. If you do hear a beep when you try to launch, recognize instantly that you must wait to do so. You must reposition your cursor, watch for the first of your ABM clouds to vanish, and then fire. Hopefully, you will not be too late. Some players, on the other hand, try to plan their shots so that they can space them evenly; by so doing, they can maintain a continuous fire. This method supplies them not only with the security of no beeps but also with a shooting rhythm, which is always a good thing to have. Unfortunately, in later rounds, there are always times when you need three quick shots in a row.

f. Conserve ABMs. In early rounds, you will often see two IPBMs coming together in a "V." If you aim at the point of that V in time, you should destroy them both with only one missile, giving yourself extra points at the end of the wave.

Do what you can to prevent your missile base from being hit; if you see that it is threatened, aim and fire as many shots as possible before it is hit–if you have four or more ABMs in the base. Provided you don't bring in a new block of ten, your stratagem will earn you points with ABMs that would otherwise have been destroyed.

g. You can survive with only one city, but try to keep the others for as long as possible. The bonus points they give you should be worth your trouble.

h. Once you get to Wave 7 or Wave 9, the enemy missiles fall too fast for you to pick them all off individually. You can then resort to a technique that, in the arcades, is known as "doing a spread" or "making a wall."

1. As soon as each wave starts, position your cursor a little below center and to one side of the area you most wish to protect. Then move the cursor over that area, pressing FIRE three times as you do. It is better to start from the side farther from your missile base.

2. Since the ABMs are well spaced enough to detonate simultaneously and in the correct spots, your three shots should intermesh into an impenetrable wall of nuclear cloud. Any threatening IPBM should perish in your wall, and you can begin planning the next.

i. Unfortunately, three detonations are not enough to build a wall over more than a couple of your cities. Once the going gets tough, therefore, you must decide which cities you want to keep and which you must discard. Eventually, you can protect only one or two cities to the immediate left or right of your missile base plus the base itself. Decide which side you prefer and stick with it. If you make it through Wave 13 with your city or cities intact, you can theoretically go on indefinitely.

GAME VARIATIONS

GAME NO.	TARGET CONTROL	CRUISE MISSILE	FIRST WAVE	GAME NO.
1	S	D	1	18
2	F	D	1	19
3	S	SM	1	20
4	F	SM	1	21
5	S	D	7	22
6	F	D	7	23
7	S	SM	7	24
8	F	SM	7	25
9	S	D	11	26
10	F	D	11	27
11	S	SM	11	28
12	F	SM	11	29
13	S	D	15	30
14	F	D	15	31
15	S	SM	15	32
16	F	SM	15	33
17	CHILDREN			34

ONE PLAYER (games 1–17)

TWO PLAYERS (games 18–34)

LEGEND

TARGET CONTROL:
F = Fast
S = Slow

CRUISE MISSILE:
D = Dumb
SM = Smart

j. Cruise missiles, even if they posed no threat to your base or cities, would be a significant source of points. They are very dangerous, though, so destroying them is even more important.

Dumb cruise missiles are no problem to dispatch, but the smart ones require more care. If you do not have time to aim precisely enough to destroy a smart cruise missile with one shot, you can use the more certain two-shot method. First shoot just below the enemy; when it retreats, shoot just above it. Trapped between the two lethal clouds, it will perish. Two long shots take time, so you might want to let the cruise missile come low before dealing with it.

k. With the difficulty switch set at **a**, you must always plan further in advance, and you will find yourself having to shoot low most of the time.

l. Know how the first thirteen waves get harder, so you will be prepared for the missiles' increased speed and numbers. If you happen to forget what wave you are about to begin, the screen's colors should still give you sufficient warning. Memorize them.

SPACE INVADERS

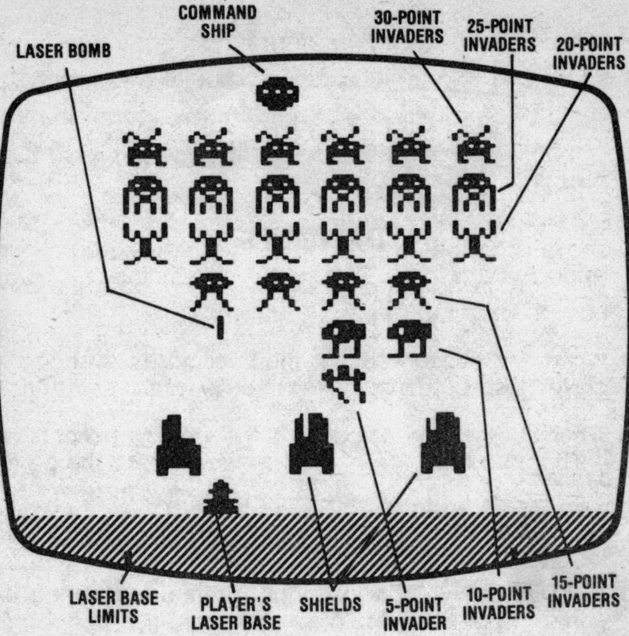

CONTROLS

a. Left-right joystick

b. FIRE button

SCORING

a. Bottom-row invader: 5 points

b. Fifth-row invader: 10 points

c. Fourth-row invader: 15 points

d. Third-row invader: 20 points

e. Second-row invader: 25 points

f. Top-row invader: 30 points

g. Command Ship in most games: 200 points

h. Command Ship in two-player competitive games: 100 points

i. Opponent's laser base in competitive games is hit: 200 points

DANGERS

a. When any invader's missile touches a laser base, the laser base is destroyed.

b. When any invader reaches the laser base's level or any player's laser base is destroyed three times, the game ends.

c. When two players competing at the same time (not alternating) lose three laser bases between them, the game ends.

OBSERVATIONS

a. The SPACE INVADERS cartridge offers a staggering 112 games, 111 of which feature from one to five of the cartridge's ten variations. Observations and strategies for all the variations are included below, but it is useful, for the moment, to know how to reach the higher game numbers. When the player keeps the GAME SELECT switch down, the numbers go by continuously; when he depresses RESET simultaneously, however, they pass much more quickly. The RESET switch can save time, therefore, for a player wishing to reach a high game number.

Basic Game

b. The player's laser base can move along the bottom of the screen, facing up. It cannot shift quite so far to the right or the left as can the invaders, its mobility extending only as far as the marker on each side. The first laser base materializes at the far left, between the first and second columns of invaders. After a couple of seconds, the laser base and the invaders gain mobility simultaneously.

The laser base can have only one shot on the screen at a time; in other words, once the player shoots, he must wait for the shot to hit a shield, to destroy an invader or Command Ship, or to vanish at the top of the screen. If the player keeps the FIRE button depressed, the laser base automatically fires one shot the instant the last shot detonates.

When a laser base is destroyed in the middle of the screen, the invaders stop and wait for a replacement, if there is one, to materialize at the left end of the player's mobility zone. The number of ships remaining flashes at bottom center; after a second or two, the action resumes where it left off.

c. The screen's three shields protect the player, although they can be damaged and even pierced by his shots and the invaders' bombs. The shields are replaced at the beginning of each screen, but they vanish altogether as soon as any invader reaches the third level from the bottom. (See next observation.)

d. The invaders are the villains of the game, and nasty they are. Their formation starts each screen with six rows of six. Beginning almost at the left edge of the playfield, they all commence a slow, rhythmic march to the right. As soon as any invader reaches the right edge of the playfield, the whole formation descends one level and starts marching to the left. When the first invader hits the left edge, they all drop another level and reverse direction once more.

The bottom row of the first screen of invaders starts five levels above the laser base. If any one of them manages to descend three levels before being shot, the player's shelters vanish until the next screen. If any of them makes it down through two more levels, the game ends. For this reason, the level just above the laser base is often called "death row."

The rows of invaders are two levels apart, so shooting an entire row delays the invasion by two crossings.

Because the entire formation crosses the screen in unison, a shot from the laser base can narrowly miss a bottom-row invader, only to hit another in the same column, producing a strange hole in the formation.

The left edge of the screen, beyond the playfield, is fringed by inch-long horizontal lines. The lines are choose set, but there are none at the level of any invader or row of invaders. At the beginning of each screen, therefore, there are five invader-high gaps in the fringe; just before the end, there is only one, usually in the bottom half of the screen. The gaps descend during play along with the corresponding rows of invaders.

e. The invaders' principal threat against the player is their bombs, which are **not** dropped randomly. When only two columns of the formation remain, for instance, bombs almost always drop from the column nearer the laser base. With more columns remaining, the trend is less noticeable but still there. Bombs tend to drop from the highest invader possible, that is, from the column with the greatest number of its lower invaders shot away.

When a bomb drops from a column, it does so from the center of the column's bottom invader. By the time the bomb reaches the ground, of course, the invader has moved farther to the right or left; how much depends only on the height from which the drop occurred.

During play, there are always exactly two bombs on the screen; that is, at the instant a bomb detonates, one more is still falling, and a third is being dropped. Bombs can detonate against a shield, the bottom of the playfield or, in the worst case, the laser base. It should be noted that the player's shots and the invaders' bombs cannot detonate on each other; instead of exploding on impact, they overlap and pass each other, courses unchanged.

Another sign that the bombs do not drop randomly is that the invader third and/or fifth from the left in the bottom row releases two consecutive bombs within the first seven seconds of most screens, often timed to delay a laser base moving to the right.

f. Although each screen of invaders commences with a slow, stately march beat, the survivors of the laser base's attacks move more and more quickly as their comrades are decimated. There are, in fact, five accelerations in each screen: the invaders speed up when their number reaches 21, 7, 4, 3, and 1. The most perceptible accelerations occur with 7 and 1 left; the last invader's pace is machine-gun swift. The four-invader speed, while relatively slow, is made trickier by its odd cadence.

g. When there are eight or more invaders on the screen, a Command Ship appears approximately every 16 seconds. The cycle varies slightly when one is hit (the next appearing 2 or 3 seconds late) or when the laser base is hit (the next appearing 16 seconds after play resumes).

Each Command Ship appears randomly from the left or right top corner of the screen. It crosses at a rate that never changes from screen to screen or from game to game; it can travel about one inch in the time it takes a laser-base shot to reach the top. Command Ships are much easier to shoot in the open, of course, than when the invaders' formation lies between. An entire screen of invaders is worth only 630 points, so it is always worthwhile to try for the 200-point Command Ship.

The Command Ship produces an eerie, ululating sound, over which the invaders' steps and deaths can be heard but the player's shots cannot. Moreover, the player's score disappears whenever a Command Ship emerges and reappears when the Command Ship either is destroyed or reaches the opposite edge of the screen.

h. Once the player has managed to annihilate the first screen of invaders, the second appears. The laser base resumes its customary starting position at lower left, and the number of bases remaining also flashes as usual. The only difference is that the formation starts one level lower.

The third screen begins yet another level down. The fourth screen appears so low that the player automatically loses his shields, and the fifth screen actually materializes in death row. The screens do not change at all thereafter so, once the player masters the fifth screen, he has essentially mastered the game.

The lower screens have advantages for the player as well as disadvantages. It is true, for instance, that bombs drop from closer to the ground, giving him less time to dodge them, and that the invaders need less time to reach his level and end the game; however, the player is closer to them from the start, so each of his shots reaches them more quickly. If he shoots again and again immediately, he needs much less time to demolish a column or even an entire screen of his enemies.

i. Unlike ASTEROIDS and MISSILE COMMAND, SPACE INVADERS does not help the player prolong his game by rewarding him for good play. His three laser bases must last him the entire game. No matter how many points he earns, moreover, his score will never read higher than 9,999, making it necessary to keep track of how many tens of thousands of points he has scored. Turning the game over, unfortunately, does not make it any easier, not even temporarily.

Variations

j. Early experimenters discovered the SPACE INVADERS variation known as "double-shooting," which results from a flaw in the program. It changes the game so radically that it could not even be considered cheating, merely an alternative challenge to the player's skills.

The more widely known method of double-shooting is also the inferior one. It involves flicking the ON/OFF switch rapidly several times before pressing RESET. When play finally starts, the laser base can have not one but two shots on the screen at a time. With such firepower, the player can demolish an entire column of invaders in about half the usual time.

The only problem is that the player's console may be damaged by such savage handling of the ON/OFF switch, for which it was not designed. The simpler, less risky method of double-shooting is to press RESET before turning on the console. Switching on the console and then releasing RESET produces exactly the desired results with no chance of damage to the console. Sadly, both methods are effective only in Game 1, the basic game.

k. In the cartridge's most innocuous variation, the three shields all shift horizontally in an established rhythm, each one traveling back and forth in an area approximately three times its width, so that nearly every possible laser-base position is blocked at least once every 2 seconds. The player may therefore find his shots unexpectedly blocked or his laser base suddenly open to attack, so he must definitely be more alert to reach the same score. After the game's first three screens, however, the moving shields present no problem, because they have vanished altogether.

l. The player can select games in which the invaders drop bombs that are either superfast, zigzagging, or both. The first type travels at about twice the normal speed; the second wanders randomly across the screen while it drops, sometimes landing quite far from where it ordinarily would; and the third can do both. Survival obviously becomes much tougher.

m. When the difficulty switch is set at **a**, the laser base assumes twice its normal width, making it considerably more difficult to dodge bombs. On the bright side, the player can actually fire from slightly farther to the right than in the basic game. The invaders thus cannot reach the right edge quite so easily as they would otherwise, but this benefit is more than counterbalanced by the anxiety their bombs now cause the player.

n. In the last and most troublesome variation, the invaders themselves are invisible almost all of the time. Their bombs and the Command Ship are not, but finishing a screen safely is still much harder. The mean varmints appear for a moment only when the player hits one of them or the Command Ship. The player can track them fairly easily during the first part of each screen, but they are more elusive the fewer remain, for two reasons: they move faster, and the player scores hits less often. The last invader in each screen is almost impossible to nail without some luck.

o. The above variations, when chosen for one player, account for 16 of the cartridge's 112 games. There are six different two-player options that produce the remaining 96 games. Three of them are "partnership games," requiring close cooperation between the two players.

1. Both players can fire, but each can shift the laser base in only one direction. Whenever both try to move it, it stands still.

2. The left player handles the controls until his first shot; then the right player takes over until **his** first, and so on.

3. The left player is responsible for maneuvering the laser base, whereas the right player does all the firing.

In all three games, the two players contribute to a common score; in the three games below, however, each has his own score, preferably the higher one.

1. The left player participates in an ordinary singles game until he loses his first laser base. The right player then begins with his own first screen of invaders, playing an ordinary singles game until losing the laser base, when the left player takes over for his second turn, and so forth. Each player's three turns constitute a normal game except that the right player's laser bases materialize at lower right.

2. Each player has his own laser base, and together the two make short work of the invaders. They still compete for points, and the loss of one player's base gives the other 200 points. Both bases then rematerialize in their starting positions at bottom left and right.

   The Command Ship is worth only 100 points, reducing its significance. The players can lose three bases between them, not three each, before the game ends. Their two bases can both maneuver freely, even overlapping at times. If both bases are hit by one bomb, each player receives 200 points, but only one hit is counted against the two of them.

3. All conditions are the same as in the last option except that the players must take alternate shots. If one does not fire within about 4 seconds after his opponent, his base fires automatically, and he loses his chance to aim.

The six two-player options each have their own special strategies, as explained in the next section.

p. The Atari cartridge is a fairly faithful adaptation of the original coin-operated SPACE INVADERS, which greatly increased the popularity of video games in the late 1970s and is still well known. To provide a measure of contrast, here are the major differences in the arcade version's program:

1. The action is quicker in general.

2. The player's laser base can move as far to the right and left as the invaders, and he receives a bonus fourth laser base at 1,000 points.

3. The player must press each time he wishes to fire; holding the button down produces no shots. Moreover, his shots can collide with the invaders' bombs. When such a midair encounter occurs, the bomb has some chance of surviving and continuing in its course.

4. The invaders' initial formation contains 5 rows of 11, not 6 rows of 6. Their values and speed-up points are slightly different, and they must cross the screen more times to reach the bottom.

5. When the bottom invader of any column is in death row, it cannot fire.

6. Command Ships are known as UFOs, appearing every 25 seconds. They possess values of 50, 100, 150, and 300 points, determined not randomly, as many players believe, but by the number of shots fired by the player since the last UFO's disappearance. (For more details, see **How To Master The Video Games**.) UFOs will not appear with eight invaders on the screen as in the home version but require nine or more.

STRATEGIES

a. Before starting a game, decide which variations you want. Find the corresponding game number and press GAME SELECT until you have reached your goal. If the game number is high, you can save time by pressing RESET until you are only five or less from the one you want.

Basic Game

b. Longevity is very important in SPACE INVADERS, so survival is the first skill to be learned; all the necessary refinements will follow.

You should always be thinking and watching, planning your next move. Dodging bombs is the first mandate, of course, but at the same time you must decide where best to aim your own shots. Learn by heart the patterns and rhythms of the game. Know the invaders' tempo, for instance, and their acceleration points, and use your knowledge well. If conscious of when the last Command Ship appeared, you will be better prepared for the emergence of the next.

These simple stratagems are merely tools for the implementation of more sophisticated ones; with practice, they should become automatic.

c. Use your FIRE button well. Keeping it down is the best idea when you know you have a target, but you don't want to miss inadvertently and have to wait for another chance to shoot. If you hit the top invader in a column and have not moved or released the button, your next shot will certainly miss, wasting time.

When demolishing an entire column with the FIRE button, the trick is to release when you see the second-row invader destroyed. Since your base has fired at it automatically, you can move away knowing the whole column is as good as gone. Once you see the second-row invader vanish, you should keep the button down only if you are shifting under another nearby column. With proper use of the FIRE button, you can shoot as many times as necessary in as short a period as possible.

d. When you see a bomb falling toward you, you must retreat in one direction or the other. If you are already as far to the left or the right as you can go, then you have no choice of direction. Beginners often find themselves trapped in a corner, hedged in by a bomb on one side and a boundary marker on the other. There are two ways to avoid this unpleasant situation:

1. If you find yourself at the left or right limit and see a bomb dropping toward you, scoot out from under it before it is too risky to do so.

2. When the invaders are low, however, there may not be time to evade their bombs if you stay where you are. Therefore, try to avoid letting the situation come about at all. When you see your base about to be trapped between a boundary and a low formation of invaders, don't let them reach you there. Advance through them instead, sliding under and away to safety. Their bombs are easier to dodge when you have room to maneuver than when you are squeezed over in one direction as far as you can go. You will soon learn that maneuverability is essential to survival.

e. Since each bomb drops from the center of an invader, you will take less risk by staying just in front of the formation, gliding under just long enough to shoot and then retreat. Once you learn to time your move properly, invaders' bombs will never endanger you.

It should not take you long to realize from which side of the invaders it is better to snipe at them. If you meet them as they advance, your path to safety is always clear; no invader is far enough over yet to drop any bombs in your way. If you chase the formation, though, you will always have to look out for bombs dropped by the column nearest you, so you have no clear retreat at all. It is wiser, therefore, to stay just ahead of the advancing invaders–until you near the corner, when you must somehow escape under them.

f. Beware of shields that have sustained damage; they are not always entirely safe to stay under. You can use shields when shooting, however, in one of two ways:

1. Stay half under the shelter with your nozzle just far enough to the side for clear shots.

2. If the center of the shield is already damaged, shoot a hole clear through it and fire at the invaders from there.

Both these strategic positions are best for shooting your enemies column by column.

g. With fewer than eight invaders remaining, your strategy changes. You have no more Command Ships to distract you, so you may devote all your attention to dispatching your enemies as quickly as possible.

You should first narrow their formation to a maximum of three columns so that it takes the survivors longer to cross the screen. Then shorten the columns, leaving only the top invaders. By now, they are moving pretty fast, so you can stand still and shoot at them while they pass you, for you could not chase them if you tried. When you are down to the last invader, it speeds up so much that you must be practiced to know exactly the right time to shoot. If you find that you tend to miss it by shooting too early, make a conscious effort to fire a split second later; if too late, fire earlier. The lower the last invader comes, the easier but more dangerous a target it is.

With each shot at a nearby last invader, move away slightly to be sure that it does not destroy you with a bomb dropped just before death. The event would be unpleasantly ironic.

The fewer your enemies, the more important their rhythm. After learning their tempos, you will be able to judge their speeds better and to aim more accurately.

h. All good players employ more or less the above strategy after the first 29 invaders of each screen disappear. What sets the true experts apart, however, is how they spend the time before that.

Since Command Ships appear every 16 seconds and yield 200 points each, a player who knows how to prolong every screen safely can earn about as many points from Command Ships as from invaders every time. With almost no extra risk involved, that is quite a hefty addition to his score. If you know how to shoot all the Command Ships you can, you will earn more points than an ignorant player who happens to survive more screens.

You will be able to bag more Command Ships in each of the first three screens than in any of the later ones, so do not let your opportunity slip by. With practice, you should be able to follow a pattern similar to this during those first three screens:

1. As soon as you gain mobility, start moving to the right. Beware of bombs from the third and fifth invaders over; if you see none, do not stop. On your way, in fact, fire two shots, one for each of the two invaders mentioned above. They are actually the only two you can shoot. The first column is too far to the left, and all the even-numbered ones are protected by your own shields.

2. Do not travel all the way to your right boundary, or your next shot will miss. Instead, stop with your nozzle just to the right of the right shield. The instant you stop, press FIRE and keep the button down.

   Your first shot will hit the bottom invader in the sixth column. Your second, fired automatically, will hit the invader just above, causing your base to fire again. Before your shot reaches its target (the column's fourth invader down), move all the way to the right.

3. As soon as half the column is gone, you will fire your first shot from your new position, and the third invader from the top will walk into it. In the meantime, you may notice that bombs are narrowly missing you on your left. The sixth column, taken by surprise, has finally begun to fight back.

   You cannot stay much longer. After your shot finds its mark, the second invader will drop a bomb headed for you. You have only a second or two before that bomb forces you to abandon your powerful position. The time should be sufficient, though. Just after dropping its bomb, the second-to-top invader is hit by the shot you just fired. You automatically fire again, of course, and then you release the button and retreat while you still can. Your shot will finish off the right column even if your base is halfway across the screen.

4. Keep heading left. Destroying the right column has accomplished two goals. It has hindered the invaders' first crossing considerably, thus delaying their first descent, and it has narrowed their formation, creating a wide

space perfect for shooting the screen's first Command Ship, which is soon to appear.

On your way left, pick off the bottom invaders in the fourth and second columns if you can do so without stopping. Once you start demolishing the left column, you will also have polished off the entire bottom row.

5. Just as you are finishing off the first column, the Command Ship will emerge from the left or right. Stay where you are, aim carefully, and shoot it in its tracks, almost doubling your score up to now.

6. You now face five rows of four invaders, all moving toward you. You want to prolong the screen, giving yourself more chances at Command Ships. I recommend exterminating what is now the left column. It will accelerate the survivors slightly, true, but consider two more results: 15 invaders are less to worry about than 20, and they will take longer this way to complete their second crossing.

7. Move under the invaders to the right, polishing off the bottom row of three while you are at it.

8. Lie in wait for the second Command Ship. When it appears, shoot it.

9. The invaders, meanwhile, have descended another level and are once again crossing the screen toward you. When they have made it past the middle shield, shoot down the right column of four. They will speed up slightly, so retreat a little as you fire, just to keep pace with the right column.

10. By shooting the column at that time, you are hindering the formation from completing its third crossing. Slide under to the left and shoot the third Command Ship.

11. Shoot no more invaders for some time. There are only eight left, so shooting even one will both accelerate the others considerably and stop Command Ships from appearing until the next screen. Instead of shooting the invaders, ambush as many Command Ships as you can

before you are forced to end the screen. (See Strategy k for details.)

i. From the fourth screen on, the player has no shields. Because the invaders are so close, he must dodge bombs much more quickly while being even more careful not to let his enemies descend. Unfortunately, these two necessities give him fewer opportunities for Command Ships. The sooner he can narrow the invaders' formation, the better.

Most of the country's best players use the following pattern in Screen 4 and especially from Screen 5 on:

1. When you and the invaders first gain mobility, wait a beat or two before moving. The second bottom invader sometimes drops a bomb right away, destroying the base of any player who jumps the gun. Once you see the first two bombs on the screen, however, you will know whether the coast is clear.

2. The instant you perceive an opportunity, start moving to the right. Shoot the second column's bottom **two** invaders, then the third, the fourth, the fifth, and finally the sixth column's bottom two invaders.

   Because the invaders are so close to the base from the fifth screen on, it is possible to exterminate the bottom two in all five columns without stopping. You must always be on the lookoul for falling bombs, though, especially under the third and fifth columns from the left.

3. Finish off the last four invaders of the right column. As in the first three screens, you have both delayed your enemies' first descent and prepared a perfect Command Ship ambush point on the left side. You are now faced by four rows of five invaders, plus two more at bottom left, making 22 in all.

4. Occasionally, you may lose more than the usual amount of time in shifting to the right; it can happen if there are too many bombs to dodge or if you dally too long under one column. However it occurs, the result is that you may not have enough time to shoot the entire right column. If

the top invader escapes to the right despite all your efforts, you may soon regret even trying.

There you are, as far to the right as you can go, and there is suddenly nothing you can do to prevent the enemy formation from reaching the right edge of the screen and descending in a couple of seconds. Your main problem is the invader at the bottom left, which is in death row. Unless you go and shoot it, your game is about to end even if you still have all of your laser bases.

As soon as you realize your situation, you rush over and try to kill the invader in death row before it can descend. Sometimes you make it; when you don't, however, the game ends in the worst possible way–a SPACE INVADERS addict's nightmare.

You can avoid such a terrible fate by thinking ahead. When you realize that you have spent too much time reaching the right side, do not even try to shoot the whole right column. Settling temporarily for just the bottom two invaders, return to the left–no shooting on the way–and give yourself some peace of mind by finishing off the two at bottom left.

The nearest invader is now five levels away, not one, and you have time to plan a new course of action. The formation drops and starts moving to the left, and you may wish to do away with the left column. The first Command Ship appears about now; you may have some difficulty in shooting it through the formation. (See Strategy I.) If you fail, consider the 200 points a small payment for being able to continue the game at all.

5. Whether you have followed Step 3 or the alternate Step 4, you may now continue in the same pattern you used for game's first three screens. If you have succeeded in demolishing the right column, simply cross and do the same with the left column, leaving yourself with four rows of four invaders. If you have followed Step 4 instead, you should still carve the formation down to two columns of four, then proceed as outlined in Strategy k. In either case, your tactics do not change.

Step 4 gives you fewer points, but at least you complete the screen safely. In general, however, you should do your best to hit every Command Ship you can, thereby increasing your final score substantially.

j. So much for the pattern most experts use from Screen 4 or 5 on. Bill Heineman of Whittier, California, employs another one, somewhat harder to master but still worth conquering. Bill should know: he won Atari's national SPACE INVADERS tournament last year with a score of 165,200, defeating over 10,000 competitors. He may also be the country's best coin-op video player. This is how he says he obtained his winning score:

1. After shooting the far right column, do not return to the left to deal with the left column. Instead, stay where you are to clear away the fifth column, now the farthest to the right.

2. If successful, meet the oncoming formation and exterminate the fourth column and then the third. The survivors will accelerate, of course, so you must be quick.

3. Only ten invaders now remain, and the first Command Ship is due any second. You can kill the two at bottom left, keeping eight in order to ambush more Command Ships before the screen ends. When Bill is in a hurry for points, he sometimes forgoes such niceties and finishes the whole screen without hunting for Command Ships. When the next screen appears, he does the same thing again, and he says that each one takes him only 20-25 seconds.

Choose your own pace. If you are entirely sure of your survival skills, Bill's method is the quickest way to score; if not, then the conventional pattern is more secure. With it, you need to take less risk for every thousand points, and there are certainly more chances to relax from the hectic, wearying, constant movement required by the first few seconds of every screen. In short, either method can prove effective, depending on your stylistic strengths and your frame of mind. It is useful at least to be aware of both.

k. In every screen, you wind up with two columns of four invaders. Here are a few tactics for bagging as many Command Ships as possible during the final part of the screen:

1. After shooting one Command Ship, start planning for the next. Observe your position in regard to the invaders and notice in which direction they are moving. You can deduce where they will be when the next Command Ship appears; then you will know the right place for your own base, the location that will give you the clearest shots and best chances at your target. Once you know where you want to be, you have a limited amount of time to get there, so you had better begin.

2. The maneuver often requires shifting under the advancing invaders. Since there are only two columns, it should not be too difficult. Simply meet them as they advance, drawing the fire of the closer column. When you see two bombs in the air, you know it is safe for you to dart under the second column and then through, not waiting for their march to carry them past you.

3. Be prepared for the Command Ship to emerge from either side. When it does, give yourself as many chances at it as you can.

4. You should shoot as soon as the ship is one inch to the left or right of you (on a 19-inch screen). Then retreat about an inch and a half so that you can fire again if you see your first shot miss by a hair; follow the same procedure with your second shot. With practice, you should almost never miss on a clear shot, but it does no harm to make sure.

5. When the invaders come lower, make especially sure that you do not get trapped between them and the side while awaiting a Command Ship. The situation can end happily but, if the ship emerges from behind the invaders rather than from behind you, you may have to wait too long for it to reach you. In that case, you must choose between giving up on the ship and risking destruction by the invaders. It is much better to slip under your enemies beforehand, while you still have the chance. You will then be prepared for a Command Ship from either side.

6. Once the invaders reach death row, it is time to end the screen. Do so as neatly and as quickly as possible. (See Strategy g.) To avoid any stray bombs, remember to retreat before them as you pick them off.

l. Sometimes you will have to shoot at a Command Ship through the enemy formation. The endeavor is not easy, but here are the steps to follow:

1. Observe the Command Ship's direction and velocity.

2. Pick an aisle between two columns. It should be the one closest to the ship, which will still give you time for preparation without risk.

3. Move to the chosen aisle. Position your nozzle in the left half of the aisle if the invaders are moving left, in the right half if they are moving right. While you wait for the ship, shift to maintain your position relative to the formation. Beware of bombs.

4. Shoot when the time is right. If possible, move to a backup position for another chance in case you miss. As long as you are careful, there is nothing wrong with chasing Command Ships. Since you can exterminate the invaders when you feel like it, you have nothing better to do with your time meanwhile.

m. Because the invaders in the game's coin-operated version cannot fire when in the second level from the bottom, arcade experts have developed an effective "death row method" that allows them to play indefinitely. (See **How To Master the Video Games.**) Unfortunately, you cannot exploit that quirk in the program at home, because it has been removed. Still, the SPACE INVADERS cartridge's basic game offers enough loopholes for a skillful player to master it and to play as long as his fingers and interest endure.

Variations

n. When double-shooting, you can do more than just shoot invaders more quickly. You can try for each Command Ship twice as many times before it vanishes, but you must change your moving and firing rhythms somewhat.

With only eight invaders remaining, you must keep your extra firepower in mind, because you might accidentally shoot one of them and end the screen prematurely. The double-shooting player requires no new strategies, but he must work out some slightly different maneuvering and firing patterns to take advantage of his base's increased capabilities.

o. When you choose a game with moving shields, you need more of a sense of rhythm than ever. You must know when the shields will protect you and when they will expose you, when they will block you and when they will give you openings.

You need worry only during the first three screens, of course, since they disappear after that. One effective stratagem during each of those first three screens is to let one of the bottom-row invaders survive until it comes low enough for the troublesome shields to vanish. Before that occurs, you must always take the shields into account when planning any move. Timing is essential.

p. You must adjust your strategy somewhat to the fast bombs and the wide laser base (difficulty switch set at **a**). Instead of shooting at each invader's center, try to nick it on the side, reducing the risk of being hit yourself. Apart from that, simply try to accomplish what you can with your handicaps, using most of the basic game's strategies. This variation, although frustrating, can even be good training toward mastery of the basic game.

The zigzagging bombs, however, introduce a new element of luck that changes the game completely. You must watch every bomb that drops near you. Imagine a "V" with your laser base at the point; any bomb within the "V" is dangerous. If the bomb nears the ground and is still close to you, you must take evasive action. Even so, the random wanderings of the bombs make the end of the game just a matter of time.

q. You cannot do well against the invisible invaders until you have mastered the basic game, and even then it is hard. You will shoot enough invaders in the first part of each screen to know their whereabouts at all times, but the last few are more difficult, and the final survivor is extremely challenging. Experienced players use two indicators to pinpoint its position: the gap in the fringe on the screen's left edge (Observation d) reveals the invader's level, and its bombs show its horizontal position. End each screen as quickly as possible: you will have fewer chances at Command Ships, but you will also have more opportunities to stop the last invader from ending the game for you.

r. In all three of the partnership options, the first step is to find someone who knows the same patterns you do. Since patterns like those above have been shown to produce the most points, your score together will depend on how well you can both act as a single player. If the two of you start operating at cross-purposes, you will miss opportunities or even lose a laser base. Each of you has less to concentrate on than ordinarily, but you will fail if your actions are not directed toward precisely the same goals. All three options are designed to make teamwork absolutely necessary.

s. In the alternating competitive option, play for points normally; your opponent's performance and yours have no influence on each other, since the scores are compared only when both of you have finished. Just do as well as you can. The bottom right corner is a somewhat superior starting position, especially in later screens, so take your turn second whenever possible.

t. When choosing the option in which both of you are on the screen shooting and maneuvering at the same time, there is one point you must clarify immediately: how important is winning to each of you? The two of you can work together to get through as many screens as possible, not caring much who has more points at the end, or you can play more against each other than against the invaders, often ending the game deliberately within five screens. If you decide to play cooperatively, your two bases should get through many screens together. One of you starts on the right, so he can take care of the two or three far-right columns by himself. The other can attack the left bottom rows, although he must be very careful in later screens. One reason you can play for so long is that with two players you lack the sense of urgency that in singles often causes carelessness and mishaps.

Command Ships are still worth trying for, although each one is now worth less than a column of invaders. When both of you have clear shots, the one closer to the ship when it appears will usually get the 100 points.

u. When you play to beat your opponent, other aspects of the game gain importance. You should always try to be the player on the right, because your position is by far the safer in later screens. If your opponent catches on, though, and demands to be on the right half the time, your position on the left is not entirely hopeless. Although it may be risky in later screens to cross under the invaders to the right, you can carve a niche for yourself by eliminating the second column from the left as soon as possible. You will then be able to attack the first column as it advances, precisely what your opponent is doing on your right. Once each of you has finished two columns, your adversary will have to be quick to survive under the remaining two, which will be right on top of him. Once he has gotten rid of the difficult bottom rows, you can slide over and collect bigger points by finishing off the top rows.

These are just the bare bones of a strategy, of course; you must model your tactics according to your adversary's abilities. Once you have acquired a substantial lead, you may wish to end the game by permitting the invaders to reach your level. You can, for instance, refuse to shoot the last invader after your opponent misses it. The game is over, and you win.

From the fifth screen on, you can make your opponent shoot all the bottom-row invaders, taking the more valuable ones yourself. If he is losing, he will want to keep the game going, so he will be forced to take all the risks. Meanwhile, the difference between your scores increases with every screen.

v. The strategies for the competitive option with alternating shots are like those described above, only more so. If you decide to work together against the invaders, you should each shoot as soon as possible. Each player should be sure not to place himself in a dangerous position hoping to shoot his way out of it, because he will have no firepower for several seconds if his partner happens to fire at the

GAME VARIATIONS

BASIC GAME	ALTERNATING TURNS	COMPETING AT SAME TIME	COMPETING AT SAME TIME ALTERNATING SHOTS	ONE PLAYER MOVES RIGHT ONE PLAYER MOVES LEFT	ALTERNATING FIRING & CONTROL	ONE PLAYER MOVES ONE PLAYER FIRES				
1	17	33	49	65	81	97				
2	18	34	50	66	82	98	MS			
3	19	35	51	67	83	99		ZB		
4	20	36	52	68	84	100	MS	ZB		
5	21	37	53	69	85	101			FB	
6	22	38	54	70	86	102	MS		FB	
7	23	39	55	71	87	103		ZB	FB	
8	24	40	56	72	88	104	MS	ZB	FB	
9	25	41	57	73	89	105				IN
10	26	42	58	74	90	106	MS			IN
11	27	43	59	75	91	107		ZB		IN
12	28	44	60	76	92	108	MS	ZB		IN
13	29	45	61	77	93	109			FB	IN
14	30	46	62	78	94	110	MS		FB	IN
15	31	47	63	79	95	111		ZB	FB	IN
16	32	48	64	80	96	112	MS	ZB	FB	IN
ONE PLAYER	TWO OPPOSING PLAYERS			TWO-PLAYER PARTNERSHIPS						

LEGEND

MS: = Moving Shields
ZB: = Zigzagging Bombs
FB: = Fast Bombs
IN: = Invisible Invaders

wrong time, sending a shot toward the top of the screen rather than toward an invader. Time your shots carefully but keep in mind that, the sooner each of you fires, the more shots you can aim at the invaders before they come too low. Because of your two bases' interdependence, working together in this option requires almost as much teamwork as the so-called partnership options.

If you are playing purely competitively, though, the game becomes much more complicated. You need all the tactics described in Strategy u plus some new ones. When you see your opponent in a dangerous position and you know he wants to fire, delay him as long as possible. He will often either get hit or have to retreat. When you finally do fire, you will be in the position of your choice, whereas he may be unable to find a target.

There are other ways of using your ability to render him temporarily powerless. Observe his style and take advantage of his weaknesses. The room for strategy is infinite.

When you have accumulated a sizable lead and wish to end the game in an advanced screen, it is very simple no matter which side of the screen you start on. Just delay all your shots as long as possible and miss deliberately when you do shoot. If you are on the right, the invaders will have nothing to stop them from reaching the right edge and descending, and your opponent will not have time to shoot every one of the bottom-row invaders. To avoid being hit, though, you may wish to shoot the bottom right invader.

If you start on the left, your opponent will be hard pressed to get the whole right column by himself before it leaves his range. Furthermore, the bottom row will remain intact. You must be able, though, to slide along between two columns, keeping pace with them so as not to be hit. The game will end, with you the winner.

The competitive options of SPACE INVADERS involve the same battlefield but a different battle.

WARLORDS

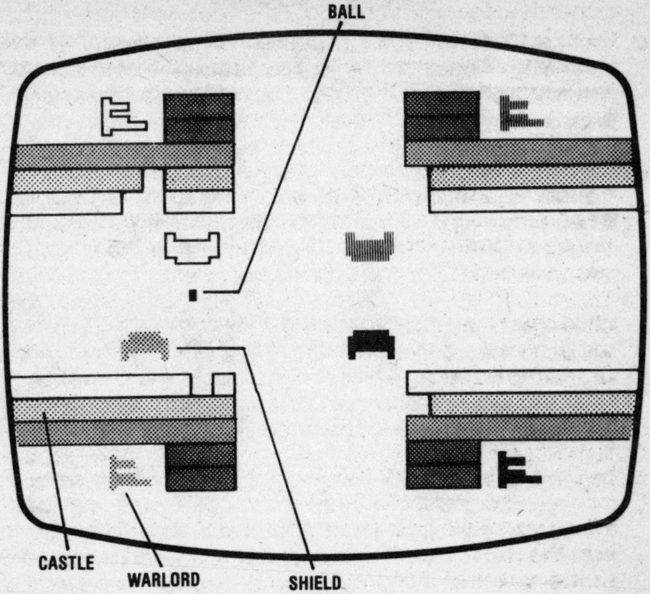

CONTROLS

a. Two-directional dial

b. CATCH button

SCORING

a. One point for being the last warlord alive after a battle.

b. The first player with five points wins the game.

DANGERS

a. If the ball strikes the player's warlord, that warlord is out of the battle but not out of the game.

OBSERVATIONS

a. Each warlord occupies a corner of the screen. At the beginning of each battle, he is protected on both sides by a sturdy castle consisting of 21 blocks of stone, three stones thick at every point.

b. The WARLORDS cartridge gives players the choice of fireballs or lightning balls, of which the latter are quicker. When either type of ball hits a castle wall, it knocks out a block and then rebounds away. The darker the block hit, the faster the ball moves afterward.

If two blocks are touching only at their corners, the ball may sometimes slip between them, hitting either another block or an empty space. When enough blocks in one section of his castle wall have been knocked out, the warlord himself becomes vulnerable to the deadly ball.

c. The warlord's only defense is his shield, which he can maneuver along the outside of the castle wall. The shield moves vertically in one part of its circuit and horizontally in the other. Whenever it is protecting the horizontal segment of the wall, the shield faces up or down; whenever it is protecting the vertical segment, it faces left or right. At the corner of its circuit, though, when it is nearest the center of the screen, the shield faces diagonally across the screen.

The player's dial moves the shield clockwise and counter-clockwise. When a ball strikes the shield, the direction in which it rebounds off involves two factors:

1. The direction from which the ball came.

2. Where on the shield the ball hit. If a ball hits the player's shield in a certain place from a certain angle, it will always bounce off the same way (unless the player catches it, as described in Observation e).

d. The cartridge offers games for from one to four players. A lone player occupies the castle at top left, struggling against three computer-controlled shields. If a second player joins, he takes the castle at bottom right. In another two-player variation, each player controls two shields with one dial, protecting both castles on the left or right side.

An extra pair of dials is required for more than two players. The third player takes the castle at top right, leaving only the bottom left to the computer; a fourth player occupies that last corner.

There is also a young children's variation for two to four players in which the game's pace is much slower.

e. In games with the CATCH variation, the player can do more than just bounce the ball away. By depressing the red button on his controller before the ball strikes his shield, he can actually catch the ball, not letting it go until he releases the button.

When the ball is released, it flies off in whichever direction the shield is facing; in other words, each player can send balls in only three directions after catching them, since his shield can face in only three directions. The ball always travels fast when released.

f. When the player is pressing the CATCH button and a ball hits the castle and bounces into the backside of a shield, the ball sticks. When the player is not pressing CATCH or is playing in a game without CATCH, the ball ricochets off the back of the shield toward the castle, doing more damage.

g. Each computer-controlled shield tracks the ball in the following manner; take as an example the bottom left shield. When the ball is in the bottom of the screen, the shield follows its vertical coordinate, that is, it moves to stay at the same height as the ball. When the ball is in the leftmost part of the screen, the shield follows its horizontal coordinate. When the ball is neither in the bottom nor in the left, the shield stands still at the corner of its circuit.

The computer's shields are easy opponents. They all move much more slowly horizontally than vertically. Although they can catch the ball and release it in unexpected directions, they occasionally release it backward, damaging their own castles or even destroying their own warlords.

h. Once a warlord is destroyed, he and his shield vanish until the next battle. They leave "ghosts" behind, though, shadowy images that periodically flash into visibility. Ghosts of the player-controlled warlords and shields are unimportant, but the computer's vanished shields can still influence the battle's outcome. They follow the ball just as though they were still in the battle, and sometimes they even deflect it.

i. The arcade version, a popular Atari product, is different in several respects:

1. The computer always controls at least two shields.
2. The game ends as soon as the player loses one battle, and the fireballs increase speed from battle to battle.
3. There are no ghosts, but each of the computer's warlords shoots forth an extra fireball when destroyed. By the end of the battle, there can be four fireballs on the screen at once.
4. The player can release the ball at many different angles after catching it, depending on where his shield is stationed. He cannot keep it too long, though, since the fireball throws out flames that begin to damage the player's castle wall.

All in all, arcade WARLORDS is more difficult than the home version's singles game, although playing against friends on the TV is a different story.

STRATEGIES

a. In games without CATCH, WARLORDS is a totally defensive game in which the player's success depends solely on his reflexes. Winning with CATCH requires more planning, much of which is explained in the strategies below.

b. Learn the game using fireballs or the children's version. Once you know how the dials, shields, and ricochets work, you may wish to move on to the faster, more exciting lightning balls.

c. Before starting your training, you should pick one of the four castles to learn and then stick with it, strengthening your skills until you are good enough to play in any corner. The top left castle is as good as any to start with since, you can occupy it in any game the cartridge offers.

d. Without an understanding of the WARLORDS rebound angles, you will never be able to defeat experienced opponents. The second the ball leaves any shield, you should know exactly where it is going and how much of a threat or opportunity it represents to you.

e. If you know the habits of computer-controlled shields after they vanish, you can use the ghosts to defeat your remaining opponents, human or computerized. In a given situation, a computer ghost will always deflect the ball the same way. You can incorporate such predictable deflections into your planning, attacking a computerized warlord from a new angle or catching a human one by surprise. If the ghost you use is above or below you, however, you must be sure that you let it catch up with you before you release the ball. If the ghost is not across from you at the proper time, all your planning will have been purposeless.

f. Thanks to CATCH, there is a considerable element of calculation involved in WARLORDS. You can catch the ball and release it from a large but finite number of points along your shield's circuit. Some spots are more promising than others, and timing is an important factor.

Experiment to find the shots you prefer. Build up a repertoire so that you can dazzle computer and friends alike with the speed and variety of your attack. To start you off, here are four shots that Bill Heineman finds particularly effective. They work from any corner, but the following diagram on page 74 takes the top left castle as the point of origin:

1. Slide to the corner of your circuit, make sure you are facing the opposite corner, then fire. Ultimately, you threaten a human opponent at bottom left.

2. This shot can be effective against two of your adversaries. If the bottom left warlord and the top right warlord

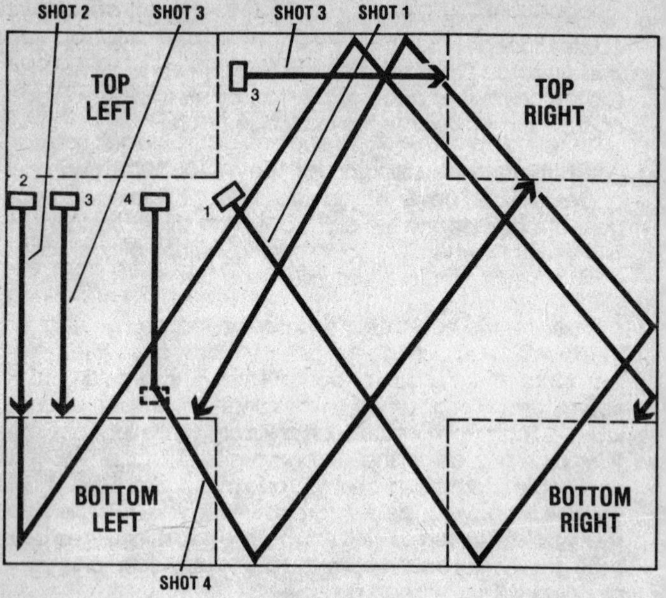

are both out of the battle, the bottom right warlord will have to be most alert to protect his castle.

3. Human opponents tend to overreact when taken by surprise. If you suddenly slide all the way to one extremity of your shield's circuit or the other, the warlord you are threatening will automatically slide his shield as far as possible in that direction, probably turning his dial more than necessary. Before releasing, however, you have already moved back an inch. Even if he sees what you have done, he cannot react in time to stop the ball from hurtling past him into his castle.

4. This complicated shot is equally effective against human opponents and the computer. Use it against the warlord at the top right and only if the one at the bottom left has been destroyed.

Start at the corner of your shield's circuit, diverting your opponent's suspicions. Then shift to the left about two inches, give the ghost shield a second to catch up with you, and let fly. The ghost shield will deflect it to the bottom wall, from which it will rebound past the bottom right warlord's territory to chip away at the top right castle. If you succeed several times in one battle, in fact, you can hit the top right warlord himself with the same shot.

g. With practice, you should be able to win a game against the computer's three warlords in five short battles. The computers, unlike human opponents, do not learn from experience, so you can win every battle with the following pattern:

1. Catch the ball as soon as you can, slide quickly all the way to the left, and release.

2. The bottom left shield moves too slowly to intercept your shot, which therefore knocks out the castle's top left block. The ball then rebounds up and to the right.

3. Catch it before it can hit your own castle. Then repeat Step 1 three times, destroying the bottom left warlord.

4. The ball will bounce around by itself for a while, clearing away most of the bottom left castle, and then travel to the top right. The next time you can catch it, start chipping away at the top right castle.

5. This campaign is trickier than the first since the computer's shields all react quickly vertically–but still not too challenging. It involves the repetition of one good shot until the warlord is destroyed.

   Bring your shield and the ball as far counter clockwise as possible with the enemy shield facing down. If you move an iota counterclockwise, the enemy shield will start facing right. For some reason, this has proved to be the best position from which to start this particular attack.

   When you feel ready, streak to the top of the screen and release the ball the instant you arrive–no sooner, no later. The enemy shield should catch up with you just a moment too late, letting the ball chip away the castle's top left block. Once you have the maneuver down, the computer is easy to trick; four successful tries are enough to destroy the top right warlord.

6. Now you can devote all your attention to finishing off your last enemy. Whenever you catch the ball from now on, slide quickly to the left and release, accomplishing Shot 2 in the above diagram.

   You must slide to the left and fire quickly to prevent the ghost of the bottom left shield from catching up with you and deflecting the shot. You may need to make the shot a few times just to clear away rubble remaining from the two devastated castles, but then you should be able to finish the battle in just a few quick shots, since the bottom right shield moves horizontally so slowly.

7. For some reason, the bottom right warlord seems to be the most suicidal of all three enemies. In some battles, his shield will catch the ball before you have a chance to vanquish the villian at top right, and the shield will keep shooting the ball backward until it eventually hits the warlord.

   When facing the top right warlord last, you can either follow your usual pattern of going for the top left of his castle, or you can ruin him with Shot 4 in the diagram. Both methods are effective, but the latter provides variety.

   Whether you finish with the top or bottom right opponent, each battle against the three computer warlords should last less than 2 minutes.

h. When playing against one or more friends, know their styles. You can exploit their weaknesses and deal with their strengths better once you have used observation and experimentation. If one shot of yours always fails against a particular friend, for example, either improve the shot or abandon it altogether, trying others until you find at least three or four chinks in his armor.

   If you see that he almost always reacts to certain stimuli in the same way, you can easily find a good way to fake him out, but don't do it so often that he figures out your strategy.

GAME VARIATIONS

GAME NO.	PLAYERS	SHIELDS	BALL SPEED
1	4	C	F
2	3	C	F
3	2	C	F
4	1	C	F
5	D	C	F
6	4	C	S
7	3	C	S
8	2	C	S
9	1	C	S
10	D	C	S
11	4	R	F
12	3	R	F
13	2	R	F
14	1	R	F
15	D	R	F
16	4	R	S
17	3	R	S
18	2	R	S
19	1	R	S
20	D	R	S
21	4	R	S
22	3	R	S
23	2	R	S

Games 21–23: CHILDREN'S VERSIONS

LEGEND

PLAYERS: 4, 3, 2, 1, or D (Doubles)
SHIELDS: C = Catch
R = Ricochet (No Catch)
BALL SPEED: F = Fast (Lightning Ball)
S = Slow (Fireball)

By observing him in action, you can devise defenses against his favorite attacks. If you find him constantly using Shot 3 in the diagram against you, for instance, you must learn to slide not quite so far as he wants you to, ignoring his feint. Even if it turns out not to be a feint, it is easier to go a little bit farther to the end than to recover yourself and double back after reacting too soon. Don't commit yourself too early.

You must make efforts not to be predictable. Vary your offensive and defensive style constantly, for tactics wear out with overuse against human opponents.

i. Attack your strongest foe first, saving whatever computer-controlled warlords there are for the end of each battle. You do not want to fight a dangerous enemy with your defenses weakened. When you are facing three skillful human opponents, you should still concentrate your assault on one warlord at a time, going in the same order you would if they were all computer-controlled.

j. In the doubles variation, strategy remains basically the same, especially after one or both of you have lost a warlord. Discover which of your opponent's two castles he defends better and attack that one first. You can also pass the ball between your two shields, confusing him so that he cannot predict from which one you will launch your next attack.

5

INTELLIVISION

Mattel's Intellivision console features a CH3/CH4 switch, an ON/OFF switch, a RESET button, and two built-in handheld controllers. The controllers–since they function in every Intellivision game–are necessarily quite complicated, with a 12-key keyboard and a floating directional disc on the front and two oblong buttons on either side.

The various components work differently in every game, but the buttons always serve the same purposes on both sides, making the controllers equally comfortable for left- and right-handed players. Each game cartridge comes with two sturdy plastic overlays, one to slip over each controller's keyboard. The overlays serve as visual reminders of how all the controller's parts are used in the game.

The Intellivision and Atari consoles use the same type of TV/GAME switchbox, the link between the console and the television set.

ARMOR BATTLE

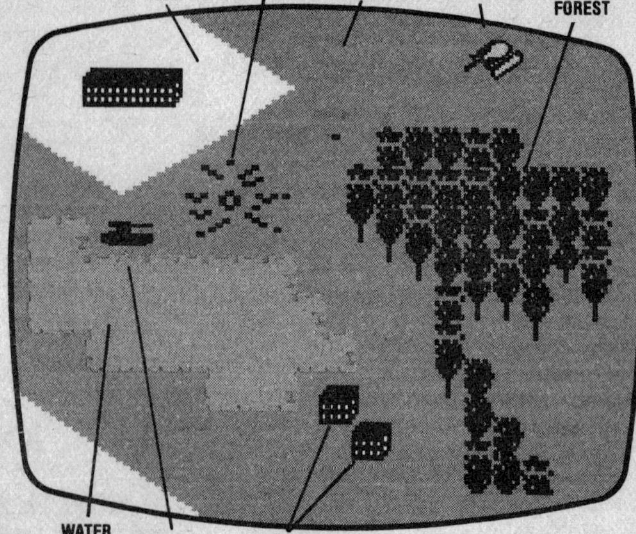

CONTROLS

a. Three speed-selection keys

b. Two-directional ROTATE disc

c. LAY MINE key

d. SWITCH TANKS key

e. Two FORWARD buttons

f. Two SHOOT buttons

SCORING

a. The player who has lost fewer tanks at the end of the game wins.

DANGERS

a. If a tank is hit by any three shells, fired by ally or enemy, it is destroyed.

b. If a tank touches any mine, it is destroyed no matter which player laid the mine.

OBSERVATIONS

a. After pressing RESET, the player can press one of the top three keys on the controller to put the following game into a slower speed than normal. I believe that the normal speed, while fast enough to make the game exciting, is also slow enough to learn by.

b. Each player begins the game with 50 tanks. He uses two for each battle; when he loses one, it is subtracted from his score. He can lose one, two, or no tanks in one battle, but no battle ends until one player or the other has lost both his tanks.

A scoreboard showing how many tanks remain to each player appears after every battle. The game has no time limit, so players desiring a shorter game may decide to play until one of them has lost a fixed number of tanks fewer than 50.

c. Every battle begins with the players' four tanks in the same positions on the screen. The left player's two blue tanks are located near the left edge of the screen, facing right. One is in the top left corner, the other about halfway down. The right player's two black tanks start out near the screen's right edge, facing left. One is in the bottom right corner, the other about two-thirds of the way up.

The only difference from battle to battle is in the battlefield, chosen randomly each time out of 240 possible configurations. The battlefield and the tanks are all shown from a slanted overhead view.

d. Just about every battlefield contains buildings, grass, forest, river, and road in different proportions and locations. Tanks can turn and travel fastest on the road. Grass is the next fastest surface, because the tanks are slowed down somewhat by trees, which also sometimes block their shells. Water is by far the slowest medium both for moving forward and for turning.

There are three types of buildings: windowed structures, square windowless pillboxes, and slant-roofed long houses. The long houses present the tanks with impenetrable obstacle: drivers can go around but never through. Only two walls and the roof of each pillbox can be seen; tanks can pass through the walls as long as they don't touch the roof. The same is true of the windowed buildings, but their roofs are smaller, so they hinder the tanks even less. Players can watch a tank through the windows of a building it is rolling through.

Shells that touch any buildings, however, are rendered harmless. They either explode against the exterior or, if they make it inside, disappear without effect in the interior. Even if two tanks are facing each other inside a windowed building and one fires, the other will not be damaged.

e. The impressive graphics can show each tank facing in any of 16 directions. The player rotates with the controller's floating disc by pressing one of 16 spots along the edge, according to where he would like his tank to face. The tank will then rotate left or right, whichever is shorter, until it reaches the desired position. If the player releases the disc in the meantime, however, the tank will stop rotating wherever it is.

Like a real tank, it turns slowly: an about-face takes about 6 seconds on grass. It possesses no reverse gear, so turning to travel in the opposite direction is always a lengthy process. The tank can turn while moving forward, although it can do nothing but turn while firing.

When a tank drives into an impenetrable building, another tank, or the edge of the screen at an angle, it slides along that surface without changing the direction it is facing. The wreckage of destroyed tanks presents obstacles as well, across which an active tank can shoot but not move.

f. Each player can have only one shell on the screen at a time. If he keeps a FIRE button down, his tank will fire shells automatically one after the other. Whenever a tank fires, it recoils randomly either straight backward or one position to the left or right.

Each shell has a range about as long as half the screen's width. If it is not stopped by trees, buildings, the screen's edge, or other tanks, the shell will travel as far as it can and then disappear. If it does hit a tank, friend or enemy, the force of impact will move the target slightly, possibly even turning it one position. On the third hit a tank receives, it explodes, leaving only debris.

g. Once per battle, the player can lay an invisible mine with his active tank, whether moving or stationary. The mine activates after 5 seconds, and he must move his tank away before then. All four tanks on the screen are vulnerable to both mines; touching a mine means instant destruction. Each mine can explode only once.

h. The player can control only one of his tanks at a time, switching back and forth whenever he likes. When his active tank is destroyed, his other is activated automatically. Inactive tanks are actually easier for the enemy to destroy because they shift less when hit and do not shoot back.

Every active tank is shown facing right. If the player switches, however, he finds that his tank has retained the position it occupied when deactivated. When the right player first switches to his second tank, therefore, he finds it facing left, not right.

Since the player can have only one shell on the screen at a time, he cannot fire, switch, and fire again quickly with his new tank. Instead, he must wait until his first shell has disappeared before firing again.

STRATEGIES

a. As soon as each battlefield appears, take a moment to formulate a general strategy; then start carrying it out. You will not succeed without a solid knowledge of the terrain.

Stick to the road for speed in moving and turning. When you

must abandon the road, stay on the grass as much as possible. The forest should be used only when your tank is in a bad position: you can escape into the trees and use them for cover while you turn around before rejoining battle.

Try never to enter the water, especially when an enemy tank is nearby. If you see your opponent's tank in the water, you can use its extreme slowness in moving and turning to your advantage by attacking it from the side or rear. Often, you will find yourself able to hit it three times before it can get off even one shot. Water can be deadly.

You can hide behind buildings when necessary; tank wreckage provides no protection from enemy fire. Buildings can also be used to catch your opponent by surprise in two ways:

1. With a building diagonally between your tank and your opponent's, you need not take the time to turn, come into range, and turn again while he fires at you. Go around the short way instead; without rotating, simply drive forward, slide along the building's wall, and confront him. Realize, of course, that he can do the same to you.

2. With a building horizontally between you and your opponent, align your tank carefully and charge through the ground floor with as little of your tank sticking out in the open as possible. He will be especially shocked if he was not previously aware that such a feat was possible; even if he knows about it already, he cannot hit the part of your tank inside the building. You can extend just the tip of your cannon and fire, automatically recoiling back into safety.

   If your opponent attempts the same maneuver on you, immediately withdraw from his line of fire and try to hit the section of his tank exposed in the front of the building.

b. When you need to turn only two or three positions, you don't need to press the disc precisely; you can just press in the general direction you desire and release when the tank has turned enough. Turn while moving whenever possible, just to save yourself time.

When you need to turn quickly to save your tank, try firing at nothing a few times; usually, the recoils will help you more than they hinder you as long as you press the disc simultaneously. This method is especially effective when you are facing a building or the edge of the screen, because your shells will disappear sooner, letting you fire more of them.

c. Learn to judge your aim: know when you have a good angle and when you don't. Wasted shots can lose tanks for you, and unjustified hesitation can save them for your opponent.

Keep the FIRE button down only when you really need continuous shooting. Firing when you know you will miss is poor strategy for several reasons:

1. Your recoil may face you in the wrong direction, making you spend 2–3 seconds correcting your position. (See exception in Strategy b.)
2. Even if you remain in the correct position, your opponent may get in a telling shot before you can fire again, putting the odds in his favor.
3. If you narrowly miss him, you will warn him exactly where your line of fire lies, and he will know not to cross it.

d. Always remember to realign your tank after shooting or being hit.

e. If your aim is good but the enemy is out of range, simply move forward and shoot. With practice, you can tell most of the time whether you are close enough or not. If you are in a shoot-out situation, the first to fire successfully has a distinct advantage.

f. Watch your opponent's active tank at all times. Go after it when its back is to you but beware of its cannon. Unless it is outnumbered or already wounded, merely exchanging hits does you no good at all.

g. You must react quickly to every situation, so keep conscious track of where all four tanks are and in which direction they are facing, especially the inactive ones. Go after your opponent's inactive tank when you can; he will either switch, attack your tank defensively from the side, or attack your inactive tank in retaliation.

In the first case, you can usually still finish off the tank you have been firing at before it can defend itself effectively. If not, retreat and go after his first tank, which is now inactive. Remember in which direction it will face if he switches again.

In the second case, you can usually evade his shots just by moving forward and continuing to fire at his inactive tank until it is destroyed and you can escape; then focus your attention on his one remaining tank.

In the third case, switch tanks before he can score any hits. An even trade is not what you are looking for. Since you remember where your inactive tank is facing, you will be well prepared for the new conflict.

h. Lay mines without stopping your tank, so that he will not suspect what you are doing. Choose well traveled locations for them, keeping in mind the routes your opponent tends to take from place to place. Don't forget where your mines are and stay away from them.

If you see your adversary taking a long, inferior, or unusual route, he may be trying to avoid your mine, but he may also be skirting his own. If you observe his style enough to know where he tends to lay mines, you may be able to guess his reasons and act accordingly.

i. These are four times when it may be a good idea to switch tanks in the middle of combat:

1. When your inactive tank is under attack and you remember that it is facing in a direction suitable for fighting back or escaping.

2. When you have retired a wounded tank from battle. (See Strategy j.)

3. When your inactive tank can reach an objective more quickly than your active tank.

4. When you plan to ambush an enemy tank that expects to be attacked by your active vehicle and so has turned away from your inactive tank to defend itself.

If you hope to fire again just after switching, remember that you must first let your other tank's last shot disappear.

j. If your first tank is wounded and you see tough skirmishes ahead before the battle can end, you may wish to "hide" the tank and bring your other into the fray. Pick a location accessible to your tank and well-protected by buildings and forest, reachable by only one clear path. If you want to be really tricky, lay a mine on your way in if you still have your mine. You will keep that tank.

k. If the only tank you have left is more seriously wounded than your opponent's, you will need all your tactical skill to prevail. Engage less in all-out combat than in a campaign of guerrilla warfare, sniping at the enemy tank from behind buildings, then changing position to attack him from a different angle. If he knows how to defend himself, however, the battle will usually go to him.

ASTROSMASH

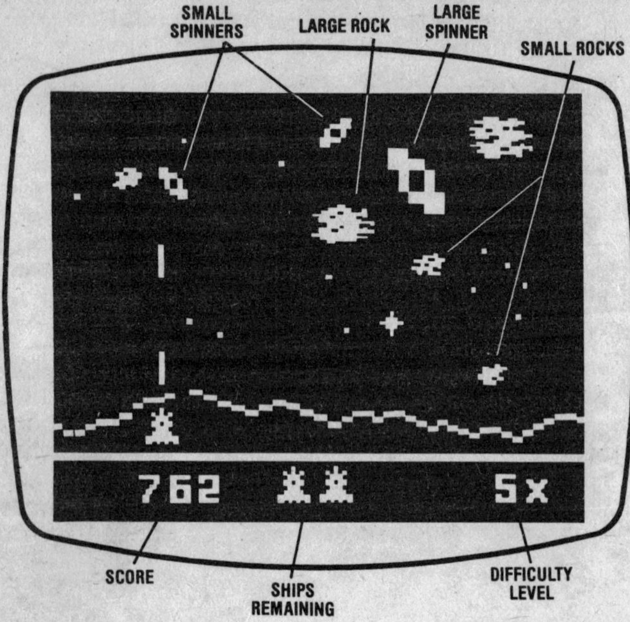

CONTROLS

a. Left-right disc

b. AUTOFIRE key

c. SINGLE SHOT key

d. HYPERSPACE key

e. PAUSE key

f. Four FIRE buttons

SCORING

a. Large rock: 10–60 points

b. Small rock: 20–120 points

c. Large spinner: 40–240 points

d. Small spinner: 80–480 points

e. Guided Missile: 50–300 points

f. UFO: 400–600 points

g. The player loses 5–30 points when any large rock lands.

h. The player loses 10–60 points when any small rock lands.

i. The player loses 100–600 points when he loses a laser gun.

j. The player receives a bonus laser gun whenever his peak score rises 1,000 points.

DANGERS

a. When any rock, guided missile, or UFO bomb hits the player's laser gun or explodes near it, the gun is destroyed.

b. When any spinner lands, the player's laser gun is destroyed.

c. When the player runs out of laser guns, the game ends.

OBSERVATIONS

a. Since the game ends when the player loses his last ship, his final score can never be his highest for that game. His score as shown on the screen changes constantly throughout the game, and the peak score at any given moment is more important. When the ship is in autofire mode, it automatically fires three shots every second. When it is in the single-shot mode, on the other hand, the player must press the FIRE button to shoot.

b. When the player presses HYPERSPACE, his ship disappears, then rematerializes in a randomly chosen location, possibly in the path of a rock.

When he presses the PAUSE and AUTOFIRE keys simultaneously, the game is interrupted until he resumes by touching the directional disc. Even if the TV set is turned off after PAUSE is pressed, the game will continue where it left off when the player wishes. He may not, however, continue the same game if he switches off the main component in the meantime.

When the player presses two controls at once, only one of them will work; for instance, he cannot hyperspace while pressing the directional disc.

c. When the player's laser gun is destroyed, a replacement soon appears at bottom center, and he can take up the action where it left off.

d. Whenever anything explodes, the explosion shows red on the screen. Anything that the explosion touches, whether it's a rock, a spinner, a guided missile, a UFO, a UFO bomb, or the player's laser gun, will explode in turn.

e. Large and small rocks fall from the top of the screen either straight down or at slight angles. The player loses no points for any rock that goes off the screen before it touches bottom. A large rock often splits into two small ones when hit. The chances of its doing so are lower the more objects there already are on the screen, since the computer has a limited capacity for display. When a large rock falling straight down gets hit and does split into two new small rocks, both follow diagonal courses to the ground. When the large rock is descending at a slight angle, however, and splits, one of the small ones goes straight toward the ground, and the other sets off at a somewhat wider angle.

f. Spinners, like rocks, can be large or small and can fall slowly or fast, straight down or at slight angles. Unlike rocks, however, they destroy the player's laser gun merely by landing. When a spinner goes off the screen before it lands, the laser gun is safe.

g. Guided missiles appear on the screen occasionally only one at a time. They are cross-shaped and pulsing and can vary their speed. They seek out the player's laser gun, destroying it on contact.

A slow-moving guided missile, when it descends to the laser

gun's level without hitting it, is capable of following the laser gun horizontally. Once it is that low, of course, the player cannot shoot it, and it is extremely dangerous.

h. UFOs appear occasionally after the player has scored 20,000 points and also only one at a time. Each UFO flies horizontally across the top half of the screen, releasing one large bomb about every second. Once the UFO has located the player's laser gun, bombs are aimed directly there. The UFO travels at a constant rate and takes about 5 seconds to cross the screen. Fortunately, the bombs fall just slowly enough for the player to dodge them.

i. When a spinner and a rock come together, they overlap without exploding. When a guided missile hits anything, however, both explode, giving points to the player. A UFO bomb has similar effects. Only a nearby explosion or the player's shots, however, can cause the UFO itself to explode.

j. The game consists of six levels. When the score shown on the screen is below 1,000 points, the background color is black; from 1,000 to 4,999, blue; from 5,000 to 19,999, purple; from 20,000 to 49,999, turquoise; from 50,000 to 99,999, gray; and from 100,000 up, black.

In each level, the player scores more for shooting each enemy than in the last. On the other hand, he loses more points when any rock lands or when one of his guns is destroyed. Furthermore, all rocks, spinners, and guided missiles increase speed in each successive level. The play becomes much more difficult whenever the player passes 100,000, 200,000, 500,000, or 1,000,000 points because spinners, guided missiles, and UFOs are all on the screen constantly.

STRATEGIES

a. Learn the rhythm of ASTROSMASH. The more easily you can fall into it, the sooner you will master the game.

b. Try not to keep your eyes on your laser gun, rather on the falling rocks and other threats. You should be able to use peripheral vision to keep track of the gun's whereabouts.

c. In order to save wear and tear on your fingers, use the AUTOFIRE mode. Three shots per second is sufficient for even Level Six, and more than most players can shoot for any sustained amount of time.

d. No matter how skillful you become, you will need all your reinforcement ships once the play becomes difficult enough. In order to get a maximum score, be careful to lose as few laser guns as possible before that time arrives.

e. Occasionally, you will find yourself in situations in which you have no choice but to lose a laser gun. Once you are certain that no hope remains of saving the gun, try to get as many points as possible before destruction occurs. You would rather, for instance, shoot a small spinner with your last shot than a large one. The more points you earn then, the sooner you can receive your next bonus laser gun.

f. Beginners often make the mistake of trying to prevent rocks from landing at any costs. If you slip under a rock when it is too near the ground, you run two risks. The rock may destroy you before you even have a chance to fire, or the impact of its explosion may cause your laser gun to detonate as explained in Observation d. Once you have defined your goals as a determined ASTROSMASH player, heroics are unnecessary. The laser guns you save by avoiding needless risks will come in handy before the game ends.

g. Listen and watch for spinners. The instant you perceive one, look to see how it is falling, fast or slowly, straight or diagonally. Thus, you will discover when and where it threatens to land. If a spinner is falling fast, nothing can be more urgent than stopping it. If it is falling slowly, however, you can take your time, attending to unfinished business before stationing yourself for the spinner's destruction. The computer often sends down fast and slow spinners simultaneously. The fast ones should be taken care of first, especially if they are small and therefore more difficult to hit on one shot.

h. Each guided missile changes course toward your ship periodically in rhythm with its pulsation. You can use this knowledge in deciding how to avoid or to destroy it. If possible, your first action should be to slide under the guided missile, letting it cross your line of fire. The farther from you it appears on the screen, unfortunately, the riskier this tactic is, since it approaches you at a sharper angle. If you have the chance, however, the attempt is always worthwhile.

If you happen to miss the guided missile, you have lost your best opportunity to destroy it. As soon as you have realized that you have missed, shift away before it can reach you. If your timing is right, it will go off the bottom of the screen before it realizes that you have moved. Sometimes, though, it will follow you horizontally. Your only escape then is to retreat to the corner. Once it is close enough to you, press HYPERSPACE. Hopefully, you will rematerialize on the other side of the guided missile, while it is forced to vanish off the edge. Even if it turns around in time and begins pursuing you again, you can repeat the process until you succeed.

Note: Hyperspace should be used only when absolutely necessary, since the player is taking a chance that he will reappear in an undesirable location. Ideally, you should employ it on only two occasions–when your laser gun is endangered by a guided missile or when your path to a fast-falling spinner is blocked by descending rocks.

i. UFOs yield high values, so destroy them when you can. They cross the screen slowly enough to afford you several opportunities each time. In order to move under a UFO, wait until you sense an opening between bombs, then slide over and shoot. If you shoot on the way as well, your bullets will destroy any threatening bombs before they can reach you.

j. Always deal with each moment's first priorities. Early in the game, for instance, when you face an empty screen, traverse it in autofire mode, thus increasing your chances of shooting any new rocks immediately and giving yourself more time to cope with whatever may follow them. Later on, when your gun is threatened by several dangers at once, you must decide instantly which one to prevent first. Remember, though, that you cannot employ two controls simultaneously.

k. Once in a while, there will be so many threats facing you that you cannot handle them singly but must maneuver one enemy into destroying another for you. When a guided missile is tracking you, for example, you can shift to place a rock or spinner between you and it. When it follows you, therefore, both it and the other object are destroyed. When a guided missile is pursuing you horizontally, you may have a chance to slide under a falling rock. By the time the guided missile can reach the spot, the rock is low enough that both explode. Finally, you may be trapped between a rock falling on one side and a guided missile crossing toward you on the other. In this case, stay where you are until both are near you. Then press HYPERSPACE. If you play your cards right, the guided missile will crash into the rock before it can stop itself.

You know that each UFO aims its bombs at you, also. You can move to place a threatening rock, spinner, or guided missile between you and the UFO, which will obligingly handle your problems for you.

l. Learn how ASTROSMASH becomes more difficult. You will thus be prepared for the developments that always occur at each stage, and you can change your strategies accordingly.

m. Once the game begins moving very quickly, with the screen full of spinners, both your reflexes and your thinking must be well tuned, since decision and action become simultaneous.

SEA BATTLE

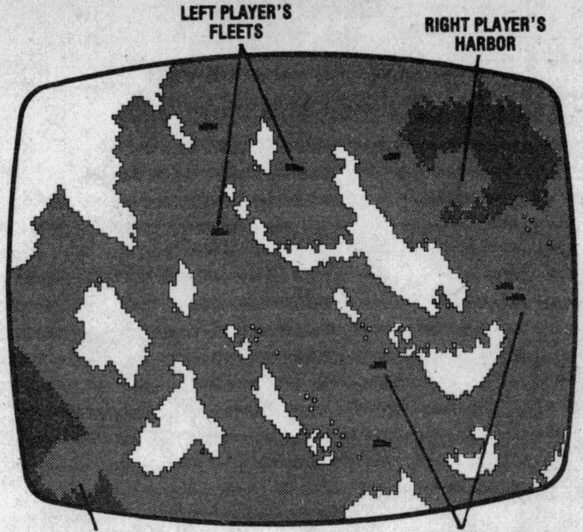

1. STRATEGY PHASE

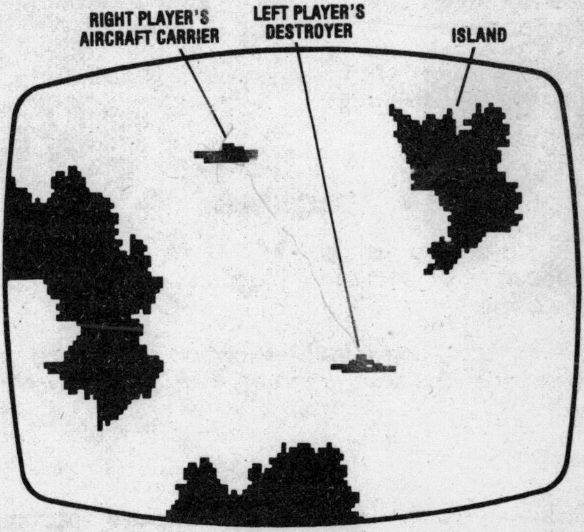

2. COMBAT PHASE

CONTROLS

a. Multidirectional steering disc

b. AIRCRAFT CARRIER key

c. TROOP TRANSPORT key

d. BATTLESHIP key

e. SUB key

f. DESTROYER key

g. PT BOAT key

h. MINELAYER key

i. MINESWEEPER key

j. ENGAGE/RETREAT key

k. CREATE key

l. DEPLOY key

m. STOP key

n. Two AIM buttons

o. Two FIRE buttons

SCORING

a. The player who manages to steer his aircraft carrier or troop transport all the way into his opponent's harbor wins the game.

b. If **both** players have lost their aircraft carriers and troop transports, any other ship can take an enemy harbor victoriously.

DANGERS

a. As they are listed above in Controls, the player's opponent's ships deliver 10 (aircraft carrier), 7 (troop transport), 12 (battleship), 20 (sub), 9 (destroyer), 12 (PT boat), 6 (minelayer), or 8 (minesweeper) damage points with one hit.

b. The player's opponent's minefields deliver 12 damage points in one explosion.

c. Running aground during the Combat Phase incurs 20 damage points each second.

d. As listed above in Controls, the player's ships can sustain no more than 25 (aircraft carrier), 25 (troop transport), 30 (battleship), 15 (sub), 15 (destroyer), 5 (PT boat), 15 (minelayer), or 20 (minesweeper) damage points without sinking. A PT boat, for instance, sinks when hit by any ship.

OBSERVATIONS

a. SEA BATTLE, an extremely well designed game, consists of two phases. In the Strategy Phase, the two players try to outmaneuver each other in a treacherous sea crowded with islands and portions of larger land masses. The left player occupies a gray harbor at bottom left; the right player, a yellow one at top right. It is possible for one player to slip a fleet past his opponent's into the enemy harbor and win the game, but most campaigns are fought to the bitter end, with all 13 ships on one side being lost. That is where the Combat Phase comes in, for only then can individual fleets fight it out with guns and torpedoes.

b. Each player can have up to four fleets on the strategy screen at a time, with one to three ships in each fleet. Except when forming his first fleet, the player must always press CREATE to bring a new fleet into existence, press keys for one to three ships, and then press DEPLOY. He will hear a buzzer if he attempts to do any of four things:

1. To create a fifth fleet when he already has four on the screen
2. To form a fleet without pressing CREATE first
3. To include in a fleet a type of ship of which he has no more in reserve

4. To include in a fleet a second ship of the same type as one he has already included

c. The ships in the player's first fleet are black; in his second, red; in his third, yellow; and in his fourth, white. The player must wait to lose or to terminate one of the fleets before creating a fifth. When he does lose a fleet, the replacement he creates will have the same color as the one lost. As a rule, each new fleet takes the first unused color, with black as first choice and white as last.

d. The ships in the left player's fleets all face right during both phases, and the ships in the right player's fleet all face left. The ships shown during the Strategy Phase do not all appear identical, but only different-colored ships have different shapes during that phase, not different varieties of ships. A black aircraft carrier, for example, appears identical in shape to a black submarine except during the Combat Phase.

e. At any moment in the Strategy Phase, the player controls only the fleet that is flashing. He directs it by pressing the spot on the rim of the disc corresponding to the direction in which he wants the fleet to move. If he then releases the disc, the fleet will continue traveling in that direction at a constant velocity until it hits land or the edge of the screen, he changes its direction, or he presses STOP, when it halts instantly, still flashing.

To switch control from one fleet to another, the player presses DEPLOY one, two, or three times, however many it takes to make the desired fleet start flashing. If he has not stopped the fleet he was controlling, it will continue to glide in a straight line until it encounters some obstacle. Different types of ships have different speeds in both phases. (See Observation p for details.) In the Strategy Phase, each fleet moves as quickly as its slowest ship. Although it is impossible to run aground except in the Combat Phase, larger fleets are more unwieldy, and there are certain straits through which only a two-ship or even a one-ship fleet can pass.

f. When two of the player's fleets occupy exactly the same position, one covers the other, depending on color. A black overlaps any other color fleet, a red overlaps a yellow or a white, and a yellow overlaps a white. Such a precise overlap is more common with one-ship than with three-ship fleets. When the player is controlling the top fleet, the bottom fleet is intermittently visible during the flashes.

g. If the player wishes to repair damaged ships or to regroup a fleet, he can do so by returning the fleet to his harbor and then pressing STOP. The fleet's ships vanish back into his reserve, from which he can then take them to create new fleets. Any ships that were damaged reappear intact. Unfortunately, the player can perform the procedure only three times per game; on the fourth attempt, his fleet will not disappear when he presses STOP.

h. Minefields are laid and detonate only during the Strategy Phase. The player can lay only four minefields in the course of one game. When the fleet containing the minelayer is at the desired spot, pressing the MINELAYER key lays the minefield silently and invisibly. If he is mistaken and there is no minelayer in the fleet he is controlling, then he hears the usual buzzer. His minelayer does not reload while being repaired, so he must keep within the maximum of four.

The player's fleets are impervious to his own mines, but an enemy fleet hitting the minefield during the Strategy Phase flashes with an explosion, and the ship that actually touched a mine is given 12 damage points. Another explosion follows four seconds later if the enemy fleet does not move away, for minefields remain active no matter how many ships they destroy.

i. The player can deactivate an enemy minefield only with a minesweeper. He must press the MINESWEEPER key before the fleet containing the sweeper reaches the minefield, or it will detonate the mines like an ordinary fleet. If there is no sweeper in the flashing fleet, he will hear the customary buzzer.

Activating the minesweeper slows it to half speed, making it the slowest type of ship and hindering the movement of its fleet. If the player presses MINESWEEPER, switches to another fleet, and then switches back, his sweeper will still be doing its job.

By pressing STOP, the player both halts the fleet on the spot and deactivates the sweeper. The next time he moves his fleet, it will move at its normal speed and be susceptible to enemy mines.

j. When two opposing fleets are within three or four ship's-lengths of each other in the Strategy Phase, the dramatic call to action sounds six times consecutively, lasting about 6 seconds. The two fleets involved flash on and off. If either player presses ENGAGE, the screen converts to the Combat Phase.

If not, all movement on the screen ceases until the call to action stops, when the fleets can resume their courses. If they are still within fighting distance 4 seconds later, the alarm sounds again, halting the game for another 6 seconds. Even if neither fleet is under its admiral's control at the moment, both will flash vigorously.

The game is capable of showing only one combat at a time. If the player's fleet enters the combat range of two enemy fleets at once, therefore, only one of them will flash during the first 6-second call to action. A second alarm immediately sounds, however, with the other enemy fleet flashing. If neither conflict has been entered at the end of the 12 seconds, the fleets have 4 seconds to withdraw before the whole cycle starts over.

k. Once two fleets enter the Combat Phase, each player can control only one ship at a time. The player begins each battle controlling the flagship, the first one whose key he pushed when creating that fleet. To transfer control to another ship, he must press the key for that ship. It is fortunate that the player is not allowed to include two ships of the same type in one fleet, for he could not then tell the computer which one he wanted to control in combat.

If the player's flagship is destroyed, control then reverts automatically to the ship he created second when forming the fleet. Even if the player shifts control from one to the other, he will still begin the fleet's next battle in control of the flagship, not of the second ship.

l. Mines play no part in the Combat Phase, but the player can lose a ship just by hitting it against land for too long. No two ships can collide, however, but instead overlap and pass through each other harmlessly.

m. Controlling a ship entails being able to maneuver, aim, and fire with it. When the player presses AIM, an X-shaped cursor, or target marker, appears on the bridge. Only if he keeps the AIM button down can he maneuver the cursor alone; if he releases it, pressing the disc moves both the ship and its cursor.

If he presses the disc with the AIM button down, the cursor keeps moving in the desired direction until it reaches the end of its range. Each type of ship has its own range. (See Observation p for details.) The player can also stop the cursor by releasing the disc; if he releases the AIM button, the ship starts to move as well. He can make the cursor disappear in three ways:

1. By pressing STOP
2. By transferring control to another ship
3. By firing: he cannot aim his next shot until his last has detonated.

n. The player cannot fire without first aiming and then releasing AIM. Depending on what type of ship he is controlling, he can use either of two weapons: guns or torpedoes. His gun fires a salvo of shells through the air toward the cursor, which promptly disappears. The salvo lands on the water at the spot the cursor occupied, not harming any object between or beyond. If any friendly or hostile ship is at the spot, however, it takes a hit.

Torpedoes plow through the water until reaching the target site and disappearing. If they encounter land or any ship on the way, they detonate early.

Both kinds of weaponry have advantages: a salvo travels more quickly and can be fired over a peninsula, but a torpedo lets the player aim beyond his target.

o. If the player presses AIM and then forgets to position the cursor before firing, he scores a hit on his own ship. If his ship is overlapping with another, however, and the center of his cursor is touching the other ship, merely pressing AIM, releasing, and then pressing FIRE scores a hit on the other ship.

p. The player's fleet of 13 ships contains one aircraft carrier, one troop transport, two battleships, one submarine, three destroyers, two PT (propeller/torpedo) boats, one mine-layer, and two minesweepers, eight types of ships in all.

Each variety has its own speed and maneuverability, its own type of weaponry and firing range, its own damage capability and maximum damage sustainable. The last two quantities were set forth for each ship in the DANGERS section above. The destroyers and PT boats are the quickest ships, the minelayers and functioning minesweepers the slowest. PT boats have the most pickup and maneuverability, aircraft carriers and troop transports the least.

PT boats and submarines are the only vessels firing torpedoes. Submarines have the longest maximum firing range; troop transports, minelayers, and minesweepers, the shortest.

q. When either player presses RETREAT in the middle of a battle, the battle will end in 15 seconds no matter where on the screen the ships go in the meantime. When it does end, whatever vessels remain occupy exactly the same places on the strategy screen as they did when the combat began. Action resumes, but the battle alarm will sound again in 4 seconds if the two fleets are still close enough.

Combat can also end when one player loses his whole fleet. However it ends, though, the surviving ships all retain the damage points they received in battle. They cannot regain their original strength except by going home to be repaired.

STRATEGIES

a. Know all the rules of the game. If you are your opponent's match in everything but familiarity with SEA BATTLES's intricacies, he will win.

b. Since you struggle for supremacy in the same archipelago every game, you should also be familiar with all the coastlines on the strategy screen. If you know which straits a fleet of given size can and cannot slip through, you will gain quick short cuts and avoid embarrassing failures at crucial times in the Strategy Phase.

c. SEA BATTLE presents so many choices that you may want to experiment with different opponents before making your stylistic choices. Even once you have settled on a basic modus operandi, you should tailor your tactics to each game's opponent and vary them occasionally so as not to be too predictable.

d. One-ship fleets are usually the best for many reasons:

1. Since you can have only four at a time, you will always have a large reserve for emergencies.

2. You can take many short cuts inaccessible to two- and three-ship fleets or at least difficult for them.

3. Each of your ships can travel at its own fastest possible speed without being slowed by or slowing another ship in the same fleet. Combined with the last advantage, this one gives your fleets increased mobility and better chances to outmaneuver the enemy.

4. One-ship fleets are the easiest to hide under one another. If you can do so without your opponent's noticing and remembering, he will bring a fleet nearby, expecting only one battle but instead finding himself embroiled in two.

5. One-ship fleets are the most effective in battle. You can zip back and forth attacking your opponent's inactive ships while he watches, unable to retaliate, and you have nothing to worry about but the safety of the ship you are controlling.

e. When creating your first fleets, save time by setting each on a long, straight course just before changing control to another fleet. You can send them to the vital outposts in a fraction of the time.

f. It is very important to remember which ships you have put in which fleets. The colors should help you.

g. You can reconnoiter by engaging enemy fleets without any intention of actually fighting. Press RETREAT immediately and evade him for 15 seconds while you observe and memorize all the ships in the fleet.

h. If you observe that he has four fleets spread out from his harbor, try to trace a path through the fleets to the harbor. If you have watched his fleets' movements up to now, you should be able to deduce whether or not he has mined any approaches not blocked by his ships. If you bring a ship through the cordon, he will be unable to create a new fleet to protect his harbor.

To prevent the same thing from happening to you, either patrol or mine all the possible approaches to your own harbor (more mining strategies to follow).

i. When you hear a beep and you know your opponent caused it, it could mean only a limited number of things. It would be cheating to glance over at him, so you must try to deduce the reason for the beep just from what you see on the screen.

If none of his fleets is moving particularly purposefully, he may be trying to create another. He may have forgotten that he already has four out. If there are fewer than four, he may have tried to include two ships of the same kind or a ship he has already deployed.

If you see one of his fleets moving with apparent purpose in his half of the screen, especially in a much-frequented waterway, chances are good that he tried to lay a minefield by pressing MINELAYER. If he is forgetful, he may not have recalled which fleet contained the minelayer. If he tends to remember such details, however, he could well have tried to lay a fifth minefield, certainly a probability you should consider seriously.

If his fleet is traveling along one of the waterways in your area of the screen, it could be that he tried to activate a minesweeper the fleet did not have.

j. If you manage to destroy your opponent's aircraft carrier and troop transport without losing both of yours, consider your position extremely favorable. It is literally impossible for him to win as long as you keep one or both ships safe. Only when **both** players have lost their two big ships can any other ship take a harbor and win.

I recommend sending only the aircraft carrier into battle, since its weapon strength and firing range are greater, and keeping your troop transport until near the end of the game, when the path to the enemy harbor is clearer. The worst that you can achieve is a stalemate, and that only if your 12 other ships are all destroyed. Your opponent may take the same safety measure, however, and neutralize your advantage.

k. Always lay at least one minefield just outside your harbor. The rest should go in the narrow waterways your opponent tends to frequent. Place them nearer to your harbor than to his; once his ships are damaged, they will be isolated and far from safety. If you have a fast fleet standing by to cut the enemy off before he can escape in any direction, you can follow up effectively on the damage your mines have caused, annihilating his whole fleet.

Once you have laid all four minefields, the minelayer is your most expendable ship. You can use it for reconnoitering and suicide missions, especially when you have four fleets out and you want to create another.

If a fleet of yours happens to hit a minefield, you have 4 seconds to get away before you suffer more damage. If you think he may have laid two fields close together there or if enemy fleets are waiting ahead of you, retreating is safer than advancing.

l. Use your minesweepers well. If you can manage to sweep one continuous path clear from harbor to harbor, that is good enough. Most players lay all four minefields in the first half of the game to pose a maximum danger to the enemy, so that a sweeping expedition in the second half is usually more successful.

When you see an enemy fleet suddenly decelerate, you

know it contains an activated minesweeper. Go after the sweeper before it can clear away any of your vital defenses. When you send a sweeper out, always pair it with a stronger ship as escort. If the enemy besets you after recognizing the sweeper's slowness, you can use the stronger ship as defender and attacker, keeping the sweeper safe in a corner of the battle screen. If you lose it, you still have another, but remember always to activate a sweeper before trying to sweep. The sweeping process is slow but worthwhile.

m. Be very quick in the Combat Phase. When such speed is required, you must learn to handle your complicated controller almost like a musical instrument. Press AIM, for instance, the instant after you or your opponent has pressed ENGAGE. You will be able to start shooting before he even gets his bearings, and every shot counts. Throughout the battle, you should always be either aiming or firing. The better infighter always wins a game of SEA BATTLE.

n. If you are both equally skillful in the Combat Phase, then armaments start to matter. Know everything about the ships in your fleet: appearance, weapon range, speed of acceleration, and so on. You will have to recognize the enemy vessels on sight, and you should never have to look down at your controller overlay. Knowledge and recognition of both side's ships are essential in every battle.

o. In combat, success depends finally on pure maneuvering and shooting skill. Duels between two ships are the most common conflicts, since one-ship fleets are the norm.

If your ship is the more lightly armored, take advantage of the enemy's slowness. His range is probably longer, but he may overextend his cursor. You can then slip under every salvo until he is in your firing range. If the enemy ship is a submarine, you must dodge torpedoes, not just the cursor, but they are slow enough at long range to present little problem.

One particularly dirty trick with a quick ship is to press AIM and then release without shifting the cursor from your bridge. Wait for a chance to slip under his cursor, then glide through his ship, firing as you do. If you manage to score two or three hits that way, his heavily armored, well-armed ship will sink.

p. If you are the one with the bigger, slower ship, remember to keep your cursor close enough for it to retain its usefulness. That means that a salvo must be able to reach it before the enemy can get between the cursor and the ship.

Bearing in mind this precaution, you may be able to "fence" your way to victory. If you can keep the enemy on the other side of your cursor, see what happens when you advance on him, your finger ready to press FIRE. With some practice, you can force him to retreat. If you repeat the process, you can eventually back him to the edge of the screen, where he loses his advantage of maneuverability, or even into land.

q. If you and your opponent are piloting the same kind of ship, the better fencer will win. You must feint, parry, sidestep, and extend treacherous invitations. Your chief goal should be to make him fire and miss. His defenses are then down, and he is at your mercy. Never settle for an even exchange of shots.

r. The right kind of player can destroy his adversary's ships with just one PT boat. This "mosquito boat" can turn on a dime and reach full speed from inertia almost instantly. The tactic it is best suited for is the cruel pointblank shot described in Strategy o; not only is the PT boat quick enough to deliver new damage every second, but also it is so small that a large ship trying to reply in kind may miss the PT boat and end up hitting its own bridge, taking heavy damage.

The PT boat can outmaneuver any other ship's cursor, and it can deliver as much damage with one shot as any ship except the sub. In the Strategy Phase, a lone PT boat can run down any wounded fleet and finish it off. The better you learn to handle your two PTs, the better your chances of winning the game.

s. Press RETREAT when you feel the odds are against you or you don't feel like fighting for some other reason. You will still have to hold out for 15 seconds before the battle ends, so it is better to press RETREAT as soon as you think you will need it.

Once the screen returns to the Strategy Phase, distance yourself enough in 4 seconds to avoid another call to action. The enemy fleet may pursue you; if it is faster, your only hope is to lure it past a minefield. If you have none nearby, get ready for more combat.

t. Once you have managed to escape, decide whether or not your fleet is worth repairing. Since you can repair only three times per game, you must be fairly selective. If you decide to repair the fleet, remember what ship or ships it contains so that you can recreate them correctly.

If you decide not to conduct repairs, do not forget the damage to your fleet. If you can keep track of the damage every ship in both fleets has received from combat and from mines, you should develop a sufficiently comprehensive view of the strategy screen. There is no question that the SEA BATTLE program lets the admiral in you come out.

SPACE ARMADA

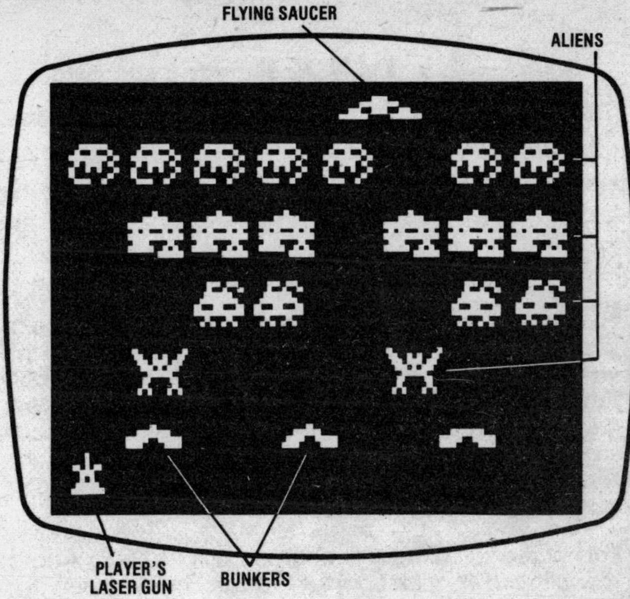

CONTROLS

a. Left-right disc

b. GAME key

c. PRACTICE key

d. CLEAR key

e. ENTER key

f. Four FIRE buttons

SCORING

a. Alien: screen number multiplied by 10 points

b. Flying saucer: current alien value multiplied randomly by 1–32, plus one damaged bunker repaired

c. Two bonus laser guns with first screen completed, one for each screen thereafter

DANGERS

a. When the player's laser gun is hit by any enemy projectile, the gun is destroyed.

b. When the player runs out of guns or any alien reaches the bottom of the screen, the game ends.

OBSERVATIONS

a. The player starts the game with six laser guns, only one of which he can use at a time. His laser gun can move all the way to either side of the screen but never leaves the bottom. It can have one shot on the screen at a time, always fired straight up. The player must therefore wait for each shot to hit a bunker, an enemy or enemy projectile, or the top of the screen before he can fire the next. His first laser gun materializes at bottom center.

b. Each screen of 32 aliens appears in four rows of eight, each row with its own color: from the top, blue, yellow, green, and orange. The blue row touches the top of the screen, and they all appear near the left edge, moving in rhythm to the right. **Note**: the rhythm the player hears is deceptive, for the aliens may or may not be following it. When the first aliens reach the right edge, the entire armada drops one level and begins marching to the left. They drop again when any alien reaches the left edge, and so on.

The screen contains 12 levels. The rows of aliens are two levels apart, initially occupying the screen's top seven levels. All the formation needs to reach the bottom, therefore, is five levels. With five crossings come five descents, and the game ends.

For every row of aliens he exterminates, the player receives a two-level reprieve. The aliens march faster, however, the fewer that remain in the screen. Most noticeably, they accelerate when only 11, 7, 5, and 3 of them remain.

c. The aliens can have up to three bombs on the screen at a

time. The bombs do not fall entirely randomly: whenever the laser gun stays in one place for more than a second, a bomb falls straight toward it. The aliens can drop bombs not just from their centers but also from their sides; furthermore, the top alien in a column can drop bombs as easily as the bottom one.

The most common type of alien bomb is white and curvy, squiggling straight down in its descent. Striking the bottom of the screen, it explodes into a small cloud of white particles. The particles do not harm the laser gun if it happens to run into an explosion from the side; but if any part of a live bomb touches the laser gun's top horizontal plane, which lies just under its nozzle, the gun is destroyed. The player's shots and the white bombs cannot collide, passing through each other without detonating; thus, if the player sees a threatening white bomb, he cannot shoot it but must dodge it instead.

The aliens occasionally also drop elongated brown bombs from the third screen on. The player can detonate these with his shots, but the brown bombs are still dangerous. One reason is that they are slightly harder to see against the black background than the white bombs. Their most important attribute, though, is that they detonate in bright red flashes about twice as wide as the laser gun. If such a flash touches any part of the gun, it is destroyed. The player must keep his gun at a safe distance from a brown bomb about to touch bottom.

d. The player's three bunkers protect him from bombs when he is under them, but they also block his shots. Each alien bomb that strikes a bunker takes small chunks out of the top surface, and each laser shot does the same to the underside. It takes at least five bombs and/or laser shots to break all the way through a solid bunker.

The aliens themselves damage the bunkers more than their bombs do. All three bunkers are located on the screen's second level from the bottom, but they do not hinder the aliens which make it that far down from crossing the screen. Each alien passes through without decelerating and even eats chunks as it goes, leaving about half the bunker crumbling behind it. Two or three aliens are enough to eradicate a bunker completely.

Aliens traverse the second level from the left, so the far left bunker suffers most from their attacks. To make matters worse, the player receives no new bunkers between screens, so he must always cope with damage left by previous aliens–until he hits a flying saucer. (See Observation f.)

The player can shoot through a bunker successfully only when his target is in the third level. The shot passes through the bunker and detonates just high enough to destroy the target immediately above. However, the player still damages the bunker's underside slightly.

e. Whenever the player hits any alien, it disappears with an audible pop and a cloud of red dust. The cloud is alien-sized but, curiously enough, does not necessarily share the vanished alien's exact location. Instead, the cloud is centered on the point where the player's shot struck, a fact of extreme importance. It lingers for almost one second before disappearing in turn.

The mysterious red dust, it turns out, is lethal to every alien, flying saucer, or enemy projectile that touches it, excluding the white bombs. If the armada is moving fast enough, for example, one alien may march into a red cloud left by another in the same row, then disappear itself as though it has been shot. In effect, the player has killed two aliens with one shot.

f. The flying saucers appear totally randomly and from either side of the screen. During early screens, they appear one at a time at unpredictable intervals and travel at a uniform rate across the top of the screen. Each crosses without stopping, almost as fast as the player can move his laser gun. Flying saucers in the first part of each screen frequently fly through the alien armada, passing through the top row without hindrance. The flying saucer overlaps the aliens, appearing to fly between them and the viewer, but the cloud of red dust left by a top-row alien destroys any flying saucer touching it.

When a flying saucer is destroyed, the player receives the points he would for an alien in that screen, multiplied by a random number from 1 to 32. As a bonus, the bunker that has sustained the most damage is instantly rebuilt. If two bunkers have sustained equal damage, the left one of them is repaired.

g. Two or four rows of the aliens sometimes start screens invisible, making it more difficult to shoot them before they touch ground. Most of them eventually show themselves, appearing alone or in twos or threes, remaining visible until shot; one or two in each row, however, remain treacherously invisible, hoping the player will forget them and let them reach bottom.

Everything else stays the same. Aliens still leave red dust behind them, they still devour bunkers when in the second level, and they still make a sound like rubbing together two balloons whenever the armada drops a level.

h. Two of the armada's most menacing weapons are guided missiles and green spinners (not to be confused with the white spinners of ASTROSMASH). These two projectiles rarely fall straight down, since they specialize in seek-and-destroy missions. Target: the player's laser gun.

The armada can have one of each variety on the screen at a time. During screens without spinners, only one guided missile at a time can threaten the player. Each guided missile is violet and X-shaped, with a pulsing tracking device shaped like a plus sign (+). Spinners are green and speedier and resemble whirligigs, turning rapidly clockwise.

Either a spinner or a guided missile will attack the gun from above if released by a nearby alien but sink to the bottom level and then attack from the side if released across the screen. If it can touch any part of the gun from the highest horizontal plane down, the gun is destroyed.

Such a nemesis must be destroyed to save the laser gun. Its demise can occur in any of three ways, all of which are important:

1. If the projectile collides with a bunker while tracking the

gun, it detonates early, knocking out a chunk of the bunker the way a bomb would.

2. If the player manages to shoot the projectile before it can reach him, it detonates early, as would a brown bomb. Guided missiles and spinners attacking from above are thus much easier to deal with than those approaching from the side, where the player's laser shots can never reach them.

3. If the player slashes at the projectile with his laser nozzle, it detonates harmlessly. The player must use a swift lateral motion to one side, depending on the projectile's angle of approach. He must also not permit the missile to touch the gun's highest horizontal plane, just below the nozzle, or the explosion turns lethal.

The same effect can be achieved by swiping at the bottom of a white bomb with the needlelike nozzle, producing a harmless cloud of white dust. Because the player can dodge white bombs, however, he seldom uses this last resort against them. Unfortunately, the guided missiles and spinners are never detonated by either white or brown bombs. They can even make it through a brown bomb's explosive flash unscathed.

i. When a laser gun is destroyed, the player's current score flashes briefly at bottom center; the number of his ships remaining is displayed at bottom right. If he has more than five left, the display shows five ships and a plus sign.

A replacement ship then appears, and action resumes. The replacement is deducted from those ships just shown. If there were four shown, the player now has three in reserve; if there was one shown, he is now playing with his last gun.

The replacement gun usually appears under the middle bunker. By holding the direction disc down to the left or right beforehand, however, the player can have his new gun appear under the left or right bunker. It immediately starts moving toward the screen's edge until the player releases the disc.

Strange things can happen when a spinner's or guided

missile's target is hit by a bomb. The gun vanishes, but the evil projectile never turns to attack the replacement. Instead, it takes one of four bizarre actions:

1. Most commonly, it proceeds to the spot the disappeared gun was occupying, then detonates harmlessly. The next projectile released pursues the new gun.

2. Provided that no bunker interferes, the projectile occasionally reaches the old gun's position and, puzzled, hovers there without detonating. The player's new gun is then trapped on one side or the other until he is forced to sacrifice one gun just to get the enemy out of his way. On the bright side, no new missiles of the same color can be launched in the meantime.

3. Instead of detonating or hovering, the projectile may continue in a low horizontal course until it hits an unlucky new gun or a screen edge, detonating in either case.

4. When the new gun really has bad luck, the spinner or guided missile continues to one edge, disappears, and emerges from the opposite edge, heading in the same direction as before. There is now no hope for the player, no possibility of escape.

j. The screens of SPACE ARMADA are never quite separate from one another. It is true that the player's score and ships remaining are displayed for several seconds after every screen, but the action does not stop for a moment even then. The player's gun, for instance, can move and fire normally, sometimes even shooting one of the new screen of aliens that happens to materialize in its path after the shot is fired. Even after the player shoots the last invader of an armada, that armada's last guided missile and/or spinner remains fully active and dangerous. Flying saucers may appear at any time, either just before the last alien is shot or during the lull between screens.

k. Not all aliens' tricks are flaunted in the first screen. The program appears to introduce one new trick every other screen, making the odd-numbered armadas the tougher ones to get used to. The first armada uses nothing but white bombs. The third is the first to add brown bombs to the arsenal, and the bottom two rows of the fifth armada start invisible. Guided missiles first appear in the seventh screen, and the ninth armada is the first to begin entirely invisible. The aliens are all visible again at the start of the eleventh screen, but they start dropping spinners to compensate. In the thirteenth screen, the flying saucers have both vertical and horizontal mobility. Instead of sticking to the top of the screen as they cross, they can dip down all the way to the laser gun's level; on the second level, they are fond of destroying the player's bunkers by eating away at them just as the aliens do. From the first screen on, SPACE ARMADA gets harder.

To make matters worse, the armadas gradually start out farther to the screen's right edge and faster-moving. The player hears the usual beat, but the aliens commence visibly faster from screen to screen.

The border of the screen changes color, too. For the first seven screens, for example, the border colors are blue, red, light green, dark green, medium green, yellow and white.

l. Someone wishing to play another game of SPACE ARMADA does not have to take the trouble to press RESET. Instead, he can simply press ENTER, GAME, and ENTER again, thus starting another game with just his handheld controller. He can also press PRACTICE instead of GAME. The program will then let him start with the final screen of his last game, although running it at a slightly slower speed. He is given six laser guns; if he clears the screen this time, he automatically faces the same armada again, continuing until he either runs out of guns or lets an alien reach bottom. Even then, he can practice on the same screen again by pressing the same keys in the same order.

Before his first game, a player pressing PRACTICE and then ENTER is given the first screen at a speed somewhat slower than normal. He can then run through the first screen as many times as he wishes until he decides to start a game. If he ever presses PRACTICE or GAME and then changes his mind before pressing ENTER, he can withdraw his first choice just by pressing the CLEAR key.

m. If two players wish to play simultaneously, they can. Each using one controller, they share the job of controlling the laser gun. It can still have only one shot on the screen at a time. Since either player would have complete control if playing alone, they must somehow split their powers and responsibilities evenly.

STRATEGIES

a. The practice mode can be very useful in learning SPACE ARMADA; use it until you feel comfortable enough to try the game mode's speed and increasingly difficult armadas.

Most important is the opportunity to practice the last screen you played. It is a wonderful way to explore the frontier. In most progressively harder video games, you must start over at the easiest level to practice the hardest even once; must sometimes even be frustrated by failure to reach the same screen a second time. In the practice mode, you can reinforce your essential skills and stretch your capabilities without boredom, frustration, or wasted time. You will be amazed how dramatically your performance improves, with each screen becoming a steppingstone toward surprises and success.

b. Whenever you lose a laser gun, decide where you want the replacement to materialize. If you need it on the left or right, press the appropriate side of the disc; release it, however, as soon as your gun appears unless you want to go all the way to the edge.

When picking your new location, keep in mind any spinners or guided missiles launched before you lost your last gun. It is best to shoot them before they reach your level; even though they are not tracking your new gun, they are dangerously unpredictable. If you miss one of them and it follows Course 1 as outlined in Observation i, that is fine; if Course 2, keep your gun where it is until its usefulness there ceases, then sacrifice it; if Course 3, hope you have positioned your new gun well; and if Course 4, there is nothing you can do but get shots in while you are still able.

c. The only way to down the armada effectively is column by column, working from the edges in. The formation needs almost no time to cross the screen and descend as long as it stretches eight aliens across. You must slow its descents by dispatching at least three of its extreme columns before you even think of shooting the aliens in rows.

The armada can cross the screen three times without its bottom row's causing any damage to your gun or your bunkers. If you manage to shoot all the orange aliens before the fourth descent, you can let the green ones come two levels lower before shooting them, and so on.

It is more important to narrow their formation first. Do not even try to eliminate the far right column before they complete their first crossing; after the first two screens, it is impossible. Concentrate instead on the left side of the formation.

If your far left bunker is solid, start with the third column from the left. When you finish that off, you can shift just to the left of your left bunker and take your first shots at the left column. After eliminating those four aliens, you may or may not have time to deal with the second column from the left before they complete their second crossing. Even if you don't, you will have delayed the descent long enough to finish them off as they start the march to the right.

After polishing off three columns, you find yourself facing four rows of five that have just started marching left again. Their bottom row is now in the third level, so you must get rid of at least those five to save your bunkers. Do not worry about shooting through your bunkers when you have to; it is for their good that you are doing it, and you cause them almost no damage.

Once the orange row is gone, exterminate the right two columns of the formation, leaving only nine aliens. They are now moving relatively quickly. Polish off the remaining nine in the usual manner. (See Strategy h, Paragraph 3).

d. At the end of at least the first five screens, let the last alien get to the second level and through the far left bunker before shooting it. When the next screen begins, that bunker will not block your shots. You can immediately slide to the left and start shooting the far left column, then the second from the left. You will probably be able to finish even the third column before it reaches the screen's left edge, cutting the armada down to manageable size while keeping it at a very comfortable distance. You will need your bunkers much more in later rounds, however, so treat them better then.

e. In general, dodge the armada's bombs instead of taking the trouble to destroy them. The white bombs are very easy to dodge, and they drop fast enough to make slashing them with the gun's laser nozzle risky. It is almost never worth it to try, for you can always evade the bombs so easily.

The brown bombs are harder to dodge because you must stay farther away from their detonations. You need considerable accuracy to shoot them before they touch ground, but the effort can be worthwhile when you feel you need to stay where you are. Usually, being driven away by a brown bomb does not cause great inconvenience to an agile player. As long as you watch for them against the black background, they should not give you too much trouble.

f. You must frequently put every shot to full use because the controls do not permit you to fire many in the short period of time each screen occupies. When the aliens are moving quickly and you need them destroyed soon, you can easily kill two with every shot, as described in Observation e.

When the armada is moving to the left, time each shot to hit the right side of an alien on the left. Both that alien and its neighbor to the right will vanish within a second. This technique is easy to master and extremely useful for completing troublesome screens in a hurry. It is almost like being able to have two bullets on the screen at a time, and it works whenever the surviving aliens are fast and crowded together, as they should be.

g. In the first screens, there is nothing wrong with stationing your gun just to the left or right of a bunker. You can fire from there to your heart's content, and the alien's bombs all explode against the edge of the bunker. You cannot shoot a hole through a bunker and fire from its shelter, however, because the bombs aimed at you will drop right through the hole. You cannot shoot the white ones, so you will have to abandon your position, defeating your whole purpose.

From Screen 7 on, you need your bunkers as protection not only against bombs but also against guided missiles, and green spinners enter the picture in Screen 11. No longer can you regard your bunkers so indifferently as to let the left one be destroyed deliberately. Never stay under any bunker too long, subjecting it to concentrated bombing. You must start shooting every flying saucer you can, not just for points but chiefly to repair damage. With healthy bunkers, the guided missiles and spinners may annoy you; without them, those projectiles may end your game.

h. It is a shame that the flying saucers follow no discernible pattern. Otherwise, you could predict their appearances and modify your style accordingly.

As it is, you are forced to let many saucers escape. The columns of aliens are so close together that it is difficult to aim through the armada. In early screens, the saucers you do hit are usually bagged in one of three ways:

1. You see the saucer emerge and race it to the far side of the screen, where there are no aliens to block your aim. Timing your shot carefully, you hit it just as it is about to leave the screen.

2. When the saucer appears early in a screen, you may not have time to slide to the edge of the screen to intercept it. If you have shot away an entire column of the formation, you can fire through the space you have created. When the top alien remains, however, do not despair. If you time your shot right, you can kill two birds with one stone. Shooting the alien at the right moment produces a red cloud into which the saucer rushes the next moment, destroying itself.

3. Do not shoot the last invader of each screen until you must; let it reach the second level in the first six screens and the third level thereafter. You will thus be letting a maximum number of saucers appear while you have the opportunity and the space for clear shots.

One alien travels no faster than three and is less threatening. To give yourself as much time as possible, leave a blue alien until last. If a saucer appears between screens, fire as soon as you can, to prevent a new armada from appearing before your shot reaches its target.

i. When dealing with invisible aliens, keep track of which ones you have shot. Firing systematically, which you should do anyway, will help your memory. You must shoot in columns and rows.

Like the Invisible Man, these aliens can be traced easily by circumstantial evidence. You can see and hear whenever you hit one, and you know when the armada drops a level by their sound or by the direction in which the few visible aliens are moving. You can tell if any aliens are on the second level by watching the bunkers whenever the armada is low and moving right.

Two rows of invisibles present no problem. Four rows are a little trickier, but you should do all right as long as you remember which ones are still there. If any top-row invisibles reach the second level, watch the bunkers to deduce their speed and number, stationing your gun at bottom right to pick them off as they come.

j. Learn all three methods of neutralizing green spinners and guided missiles (Observation h). Maneuver your gun to lure the projectiles into your bunkers, to shoot them from below, or to detonate them with quick slashes. The last is especially important for getting out of dangerous situations.

Use your precious peripheral vision to perceive a purple or green missile as soon as it is launched and your experience to react in time to what you see. When you have one of each after you, you may have to combine your methods, getting one onto a bunker and the other with a shot of your nozzle. It is nice when you can steer them both onto bunkers; if the bunkers go, though, you are in real trouble. Shoot as many flying saucers as you can and try to let few aliens reach the second level.

k. To repeat, use the practice mode. Know the game's progression by heart as well. You should always be prepared for such "surprises" as the roving flying saucer of Screen 13, which you can usually destroy with quick shooting, judicious timing, and the skillful use of red dust. Remember how the screen's border changes color, too; if the number of armadas you have exterminated slips your mind, the border's color should remind you.

SPACE BATTLE

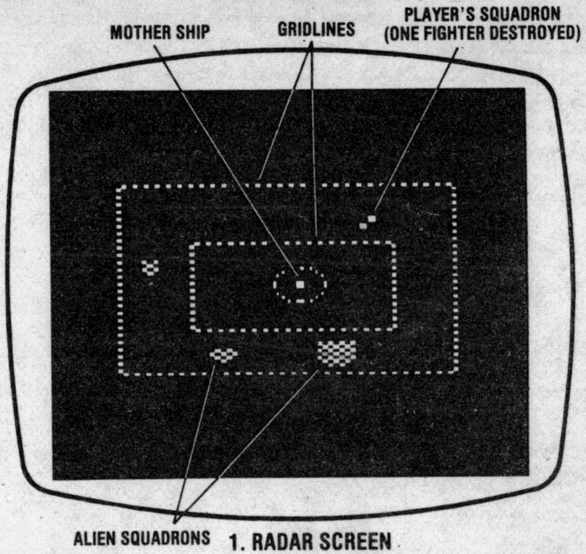

1. RADAR SCREEN

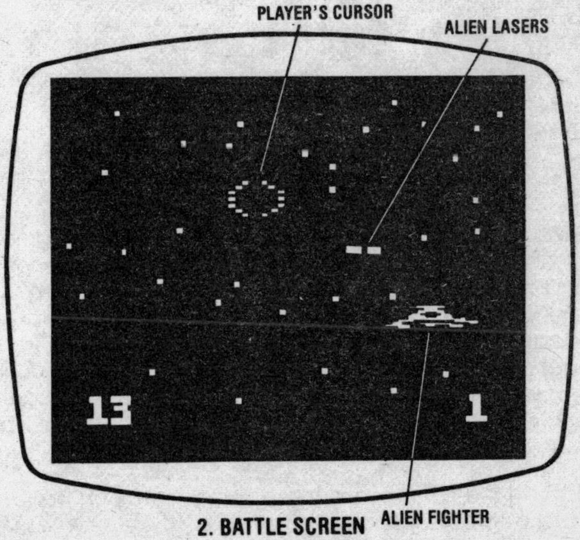

2. BATTLE SCREEN

CONTROLS

a. Directional disc

b. Three SQUADRON keys

c. Three RETURN TO BASE keys

d. Three GO TO BATTLE keys

e. RADAR key

f. ALIEN key

g. Four FIRE buttons

SCORING

a. To win, the player must destroy every alien ship on the Radar Screen.

DANGER

a. If the player's cursor touches any red alien laser shot, the player's fighter is destroyed.

b. If one or more alien squadrons fire too many laser shots at the player's Mother Ship, the Mother Ship is destroyed, and the game ends.

OBSERVATIONS

a. SPACE BATTLE, like SEA BATTLE, is divided into two segments of play. During the Radar Screen, the player defends his Mother Ship, a small square at center, from the five alien squadrons drifting steadily in from the edges. The only protection available comes from the player's three fighter squadrons. Attempting to stop the aliens from reaching center, the player engages in squadron-to-squadron fighting, starting the Battle Screen. He can switch back and forth between the two phases as often as he likes.

Each of the controls can be used in only one phase. In the Radar Screen, the player can use all the SQUADRON,

RETURN TO BASE, and GO TO BATTLE keys and the ALIEN key; all the other controls have no effect. In the Battle Screen, on the other hand, he can use only the direction disc, the RADAR key, and the FIRE buttons.

b. The player starts the game in the Radar Screen. In addition to the Mother Ship, the screen shows a Danger Zone Boundary closely surrounding the ship and two rectangular gridlines nearer the edges. There are also the five alien squadrons, four white and one purple. The player does not see his own fighter squadrons until they are dispatched.

c. The alien squadrons start at random locations on the edge of the screen and all move toward center at slightly varying constant rates. The ones above and below the Mother Ship start closer to it than those on the sides, so they reach it first if permitted by the player. The ones to the side, in turn, tend to reach the Mother Ship sooner than those starting in the corners. Only within each of these three categories can differences in speed mean so much that one squadron arrives significantly before another.

The squadrons contain from 7 to 15 alien ships, 7 being rarer than 15. The number of white dots representing each squadron in the Radar Screen does not always indicate accurately the number of ships in the squadron, for it may show one or two more than there are. The starting position, speed, and size of each fleet are random, and there is no requisite total number of ships, since that varies widely from game to game.

d. The player's three squadrons are blue, white, and gold and contain three fighters each. All three squadrons have identical capabilities; although all the blue squadron's keys are on the left side of the controller overlay, the white squadron's in the middle, and the gold squadron's on the right, the player can use his squadrons in any order he wishes.

He can do three things with a squadron, each function requiring a separate key. By pressing a SQUADRON key, he sends the corresponding squadron after whichever alien squadron is purple at that moment. If the aliens he wants to attack are not purple, he presses ALIEN until they turn purple, then presses the SQUADRON key. The ALIEN key's sole purpose is to rotate the purple hue from alien squadron to alien squadron, permitting the player to mark his targets.

The instant he presses SQUADRON, the pursued squadron turns white again. No matter how many times he presses ALIEN after that, the squadron will not turn purple, since he can send only one of his fighter squadrons after each alien squadron at a time.

If the player changes his mind before the two squadrons meet, he can either reassign his fighters by pressing the same SQUADRON key again or bring them back to the Mother Ship by pressing the corresponding RETURN TO BASE key.

Once the fighters reach their target, they start flashing. By pressing GO TO BATTLE, the player enters the Battle Screen. He will hear a buzz if he presses that key before his squadron reaches fighting position.

The SQUADRON and RETURN TO BASE keys are similar in that they send the squadron places at the same speed, slightly faster than that of the alien squadrons. As with SQUADRON, pressing RETURN TO BASE turns one alien squadron white and another purple.

e. There are two numbers in the bottom corners of the Battle Screen. The one on the left indicates how many ships remain in the alien squadron; the one on the right shows how many fighters are in the player's squadron. The battle ends automatically when either number reaches zero; the player can also return to the Radar Screen by pressing RADAR. (To detach his squadron from the aliens, he must then press either SQUADRON, reassigning it, or RETURN TO BASE, sending it home.)

During the battle, the player watches his enemies against a backdrop of shimmering stars. There are usually three alien ships on the screen at a time, never more.

f. The only other moving object is his own fighter's cursor, or target marker, a dotted oval that he can maneuver in 16 directions with the disc on his controller. The cursor moves in the direction he is pressing and continues until it hits the edge or he releases the disc.

g. When the player presses FIRE, two missiles are fired toward the cursor, one from bottom left and one from bottom right. Even if the cursor moves in the meantime, they meet and detonate in the area enclosed by the cursor when they were fired. Any alien ship touching this oval of fire is destroyed.

The explosion occurs equally soon after firing no matter where the target site is. If the cursor was near the bottom of the screen, the missiles travel slowly; if near the top, they compensate for distance with speed. The player can have only one pair of missiles on the screen at a time.

He can also use only one of the four FIRE buttons at a time. If he accidentally presses two or more simultaneously, the screen reverts to radar, and he must press GO TO BATTLE again if he wants more fighting. When in battle, moreover, the RADAR key has no effect when the player is pressing either a FIRE button or the direction disc or both.

h. Alien ships emerge from the edge of the Battle Screen and disappear off it unless shot, following a finite number of flight patterns. The faster ones often fly in straight lines, whereas those that start off slowly usually loop or swerve suddenly. The most common exit direction is straight down, but ships can go off at any of 16 angles. They all start out small, about the cursor's size, but some of those that move evasively often grow either to medium or to full size. The bigger a ship, the quicker; but medium-size ships rarely switch course, and jumbo-sized ones never do. Even better, only the small ships fire back at the player. (See Observation i.)

When a ship explodes, it sends flaming wreckage out in three directions. The directions are unpredictable, but the three pieces of debris form an equilateral triangle at any given moment. If any other alien ship is hit by a chunk of wreckage, it explodes in turn, sending out three more fireballs. However, since there can be only three alien ships out at a time, the number of explosions resulting from one shot is limited.

i. One alien ship at a time may issue a white flash, indicating that it has fired its laser at the player's cursor. The laser shots are aimed at where the cursor was when they were fired. They appear first as two tiny white rectangles; they grow as they travel, turning red about halfway to their goal. When they reach the cursor's former location, they disappear, and more laser shots can be fired. At their largest, their combined width is almost twice that of the cursor's.

The shots are harmless while white; only if they touch the cursor during their red stage does the player lose his fighter. The farther they start from their target site, the faster they travel, so the interval between firing and arrival is the same every time, as with the player's own shots.

Since the bombs are fired by alien ships and the cursor must pursue the same ships to destroy them, the enemy shots serve as both offensive and defensive devices against the player. He may find sometimes that he must abandon his target or approach it in a roundabout way, since he sees that it has just sent two shots straight toward his cursor.

j. If the player does not press GO TO BATTLE when his squadron reaches its target and starts flashing, the computer starts the fighting for him. Unfortunately, the computer does a pretty terrible job, losing–on the average–one of the player's fighters for every three alien ships it destroys. The battle can end right away or not for a minute, with either side as victor, but the casualty rate averages out at one to three. Having the computer do the fighting is definitely a gamble, and the player can either take over or withdraw his squadron at any time.

k. When two squadrons are in battle, neither one shifts in space until the battle ends. If the aliens win, their survivors resume their advance on the Mother Ship, showing on the Radar Screen the change in the squadron's size. If the player wins, his squadron's remaining fighters hang motionless until he presses either SQUADRON or RETURN TO BASE.

l. The player can choose any one of five playing speeds for his game after pressing RESET. In the first and easiest, action moves slowly in both phases of the game, and everything in the Radar Screen comes to a halt whenever the player is in the Battle Screen.

In the second and third speeds, all the action speeds up; when the player is in the Battle Screen, his squadrons and the aliens move at half speed in the Radar Screen. If the player is in battle with one of his squadrons when another reaches its target, the computer simultaneously conducts the second battle.

In the fourth and fifth speeds, the Radar Screen action never slows down, not even when the player is in battle. The aliens at the fifth speed, moreover, fire faster and more frequent laser shots that tend to overshoot the target site sightly, making them even more dangerous.

m. When one or more alien squadrons reach the Danger Zone Boundary, they stop moving and start shooting at the Mother Ship. Whichever phase the player is in, he hears a danger siren, starting slowly but accelerating as the Mother Ship's damage increases. The time it takes for it to be destroyed depends on four factors: the size of the alien squadron, the number of alien squadrons, whether or not he is in battle with the menacing aliens, and the game speed.

n. As in SPACE ARMADA, both the console's controllers have equal powers. Two players can take a console each, one handling the maneuvering during battle while the other fires.

STRATEGIES

a. Learn SPACE BATTLE on its slow speeds, moving up one by one as you gain confidence. Once you become proficient, you should be able to play every game on the fifth speed.

b. Know the rules of the game inside out; better to learn by a quick reading of the appropriate instructions rather than by onscreen trial and error.

c. Once you reach the fifth speed, there will never be a second to lose in either the Radar Screen or the Battle Screen. Since time is always vital, you should know your controller well enough to handle it in any situation without taking your eyes from the screen. Stick to the blue-white-gold order when maneuvering your squadrons; having a permanent pattern makes the game's mechanics simpler, freeing you to consider strategy.

In SPACE BATTLE, everything is a matter of priorities. Settling on an order of operations is difficult in such a complicated game, but you will have to do it every time. If you realize that you have made a strategic error, you must rectify it calmly but immediately to salvage at least some chance of victory.

d. Send your blue squadron out first, picking as a target the squadron threatening to reach the Mother Ship first, the nearest and fastest one.

e. After winning a battle, bring your fighters back to base except when there is another threatening alien squadron nearby that can be reached more directly by pressing SQUADRON.

f. Try never to leave the Mother Ship unprotected. If you find yourself in an emergency, you do not want to have to recall the nearest squadron for assistance. When the base is under attack, every second is precious.

g. Let the computer conduct as few battles for you as possible. You can always do better against the aliens yourself, and extra fighters come in very handy toward the end of every game. Ideally, each one of your squadrons should always be in battle under your command, in transit, or at the base.

If you **must** delay an enemy squadron, however, and you think you can spare the fighters, send your squadron out and hope that it does not fare too badly. If you have two alien squadrons to choose from, let the computer take the smaller, while you struggle against the larger group. Not only will your other squadron stand a better chance of victory, but, even if it is annihilated, the runaway alien squadron will be smaller and capable of causing less damage.

h. Before pressing any SQUADRON key, always make sure that your target is indeed purple. One of the beginner's most damaging tactical mistakes is to panic and send an urgently needed squadron in the wrong direction and after the wrong target.

i. Once you are playing the game at difficult speeds, you must develop an inner clock, a sense of the passage of time, so that you have some idea of what is happening in the Radar Screen while you are in battle. Learn to judge the aliens' speeds and your own; you will be able to estimate either how the screen will look when you finish battle or whether you have already spent too much time in battle. Without this chronological intuition, you have to keep checking the Radar Screen to reassure yourself, and that would be a waste of valuable time.

j. The sooner you can complete each battle successfully, the better your chances for ultimate victory. You must shoot constantly, but never into thin air; always have a target and a fallback position in case it swerves. With experience, you should be able to predict many flight patterns, improving your aiming and shooting skills as well.

Press only one FIRE button at a time; you don't want to return to the Radar Screen unexpectedly. Move your cursor away as soon as you fire. Your eyes should follow it, not focus on where your missiles will detonate. Your peripheral vision will tell you whether the shot is successful or not; in the meantime, you have another to aim.

When you see a cluster of alien ships, don't just aim at a point in the center or you may miss them all. Keep the cursor ahead of just one of them; your accuracy will improve, and the end result will be the same, if not better.

Since you now have no choice of targets, the last ship of a squadron may take you the longest to eliminate. You must therefore be extremely quick to aim and fire at it, not permitting the battle to drag on.

k. Your peripheral vision is also vital in avoiding your enemies' laser shots. If you know when and where they were fired, it will be simple for you to dodge either back or to the side, since you know their target site. Keep your cursor moving all the time, staying one step ahead of their lasers. Don't spend time in the corners of the screen, either; you can get trapped there if an alien fires his lasers from a particularly awkward angle.

Once you see the shots coming, you have two choices: either dodge them and pursue a ship other than the one that just fired or head straight for that ship if it is close enough, hoping to cross with the shots before they turn red. The first shot of each battle is particularly difficult to dodge, so begin every conflict in a defensive state of mind. Chasing the nonshooting ships works best for the early part of each battle, whereas you may need the risky direct attack more toward the end, when you find yourself under time pressure with little or no choice of targets.

l. When you think you have spent too much time in one battle, switch to the Radar Screen. You must change carefully, because you can neither shoot nor maneuver when pressing RADAR. Wait until you see a pair of laser shots fired at you; quickly dodge them, then press RADAR before any more can be fired.

m. After taking a moment to survey the opposition, you send your blue squadron out after the nearest, fastest alien squadron. What next?

If you fight quickly enough, you can make it through your first battle without dispatching any more squadrons, taking no more than 30 seconds. When you return to the Radar Screen, you may see one or two squadrons approaching the Danger Zone Boundary. Stop them.

If the menacing squadron is purple, press your white SQUADRON key immediately, then bring the blue fighters home. If the nearest aliens are white, however, press the blue RETURN TO BASE key first, perhaps turning them purple. If they remain white, you will have to press ALIEN once or twice before sending out your white squadron.

If there are two squadrons uncomfortably close, send your white one after the larger and your yellow after the smaller. Let the computer handle the latter battle while you fight the former. Do not, however, forget to return your blue fighters to base.

Make short shrift of your white squadron's enemies. If you hear the attack siren before you finish, either you are taking too long, or your yellow fighters have had very bad luck. When you finish your second battle, return to radar and send your blue squadron toward the most threatening aliens; then either redispatch your white squadron or call it back to the Mother Ship.

You have now carved the aliens down to a manageable number. If you continue to fight quickly and plan well, you should soon receive the ALL CLEAR signal.

n. When battling the aliens with a friend, you must agree on a shared, comprehensive strategy. The better the two of you can coordinate your actions at the controls to approximate those of one skillful player, the better your chances of winning SPACE BATTLE's doubles version.

6

ACTIVISION

The Activision games are well-designed cartridges for use on the Atari Video Computer System. They generally offer fewer games per cartridge than Atari's, incorporating fewer variations. The action games' rules are also less complicated than Atari's or Mattel's, but the fast-paced play and the charming graphics supply more than enough excitement to make the games worth playing.

DRAGSTER

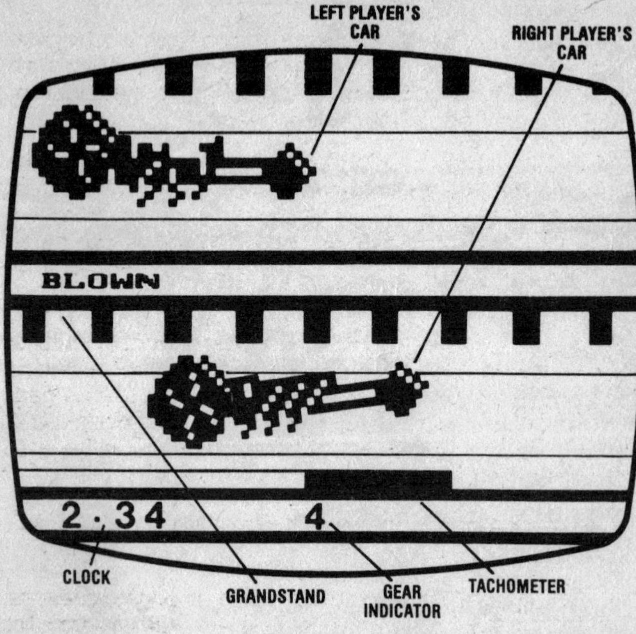

CONTROLS

a. Gearshift joystick

b. GAS button

SCORING

a. The player's goal is to get his dragster from one side of the screen to the other in as little time as possible.

DANGERS

a. If the player goes into first gear during the countdown before the race, he is automatically disqualified.

b. If the player allows his dragster to build up too much engine pressure, the engine blows.

OBSERVATIONS

a. The player's car begins each race facing right, touching the left edge of the screen. When the race ends, it is almost touching the opposite side; its front wheels are equidistant from the right edge and the car's engine.

On the way, the car moves slowly, for the race always lasts over 5.5 seconds, much more for most players. The player, though, receives an illusion of rapid movement from two visual touches: the grandstands behind his car move by quickly from right to left, and its back wheels whirl clockwise.

b. The player's car has five gears, including neutral. Pushing his joystick even slightly to the left opens the clutch; when he releases the joystick, he automatically moves up one gear. Downshifting is impossible: all the player can do in fourth gear is pop the clutch. Once he reaches fourth, he stays there.

In a typical race, the player's gear indicator reads N, C, 1, C, 2, C, 3, C, 4, C, 4, C,...4.

c. By pressing GAS, the player increases his engine pressure, which is measured by the tachometer. Other terms for engine pressure are rpms, turnover, and torque. If the player remains in the same gear, his torque increases steadily until the player releases GAS.

The car's speed is shown only by how quickly it is crossing the screen. The tachometer measures its engine pressure both visually and with suspenseful rising tones. The higher the pressure, the farther right the tachometer goes; from the midscreen danger point on, it reads red.

d. Once the tachometer, or tach, is about three-quarters across the screen–halfway into the red zone–the player hears the engine noise go up an octave. He is close to disaster; unless he reacts quickly, the engine will blow. He must do something to keep the tach from climbing farther.

Either the GAS button has been down too long, or he has spent too much time in the same gear. The lower the gear, the quicker the tachometer rises with GAS down; the player must be especially careful in neutral and first.

e. The joystick is very sensitive; just tapping it to the left is enough to pop the clutch. If the player stays in clutch too long while pressing GAS, he will flood the engine. The tachometer jumps whenever he pops the clutch, rising rapidly until he releases it. The dragster's front wheels leap off the ground at the sudden burst of rpms, but high wheelies can blow the engine.

f. The player may notice that all his times end with a 1, 4, or 7. The explanation is simple: the TV can show only 30 images per second, so the race cannot be timed by hundredths of a second. The clock can never read 6.00 or 7.00; in between, though, the player can score 6.01, 6.04, 6.07, 6.11, 6.14, 6.17, 6.21, and so on, amounting to 30 figures in all.

g. Before the race begins, a countdown to the left of the gear indicator runs from 9 to 0; at 0, the clock starts. The player is disqualified if he enters first gear before the race, but there is no penalty for putting the car in clutch or for pressing lightly on the gas. Whenever he presses too heavily in neutral or clutch, however, it takes about a second to blow the engine.

h. After finishing a race, the player can start a new countdown either by pressing RESET or by pushing his joystick to the right. If he is seated out of reach of the console, using the joystick is easier.

i. DRAGSTER can be played by one or two people simultaneously. A player participating alone can use either joystick, and two take one each. The left controls the top dragster; the right, the bottom.

Two players can either race each other to the finish or strive for the lowest possible combined score. Playing alone is somewhat easier, since another car's engine noise may confuse or disorient the player, affecting his judgment.

j. In Game 1 of DRAGSTER, the player's car steers automatically, allowing him to concentrate on the gears and the gas. In Game 2, though, the car tends to wander back and forth across the track, slowing itself down tremendously when it scrapes along either the grandstands or the center divider. The player must steer his dragster by pushing the joystick forward or pulling it back. His attention is divided, and the game becomes much harder.

STRATEGIES

a. Experimentation is very important in mastering DRAGSTER. Learn the game gear by gear; each race is so short that you should have time to try many permutations. Eventually, you will find the technique most promising for you; different players excel using different methods. By experimenting, you will also learn the mechanics of the game, the small facts that every player must know to succeed.

b. Watch your tachometer. Whatever gear you are in, you should try to keep the tach below the engine-blowing point but still about a third of the way into the red zone for maximum manageable torque.

c. Do not distract yourself by glancing at the clock. Unless you are in the process of learning the game, you will have a chance to see your time when the race is over.

d. Listen to your tachometer. Once your ear becomes attuned to the various pitches, you will be able to play even with your back to the TV set, as many of the best players can. The tach tone tells you all you need to know about how much torque you need and when your engine is in danger of blowing.

e. When changing gears or popping the clutch, you should never do more than tap the joystick to the left. If you hold it a second too long, flooding the engine will send the tach skyrocketing. Then one of two things will occur, neither one desirable: either your engine will blow, or you will recover yourself just in time but still lose valuable rpms because of the engine's flooding.

In general, the only time you want to pop the clutch in fourth gear is when your tach is low, below the optimum level described in Strategy b.

f. When your engine is threatening to blow, you can prevent it either by switching gears or by letting up on the gas. Switching gears is preferable; when you are already in fourth gear, however, do not touch the joystick. When you are close to blowing, popping the clutch is as good as resigning from the race.

You have no choice, therefore, but to release the GAS button until you are out of danger. You lose speed, but at least you finish the race. Once you perfect your DRAGSTER technique, though, you will hopefully never have to release GAS until perhaps just before the finish. When learning the game, try marking with a crayon the highest point your tach can reach before the engine blows. With practice, you will be able to recognize this maximum both aurally and visually.

g. The 10 seconds before the race starts are more important than many players realize. The difference between a good and a bad start can be two-tenths of a second or more, which is a long time in DRAGSTER.

You can take two steps to ensure a perfect start. First of all, put your gearshift into clutch. Just before the countdown reaches zero, release the joystick, putting the car into first. Your timing must be just right: you lose time if you wait too long, and you disqualify yourself if you release the joystick early.

Being in first gear right away will do you even more good if you already have some pressure in your engine. Before the race begins, therefore, pulse your GAS button just enough to keep the tach hovering above the countdown numerals. Remember how easy it is to blow in clutch, though, so use a light touch. Once the race begins, you will be ready to take off immediately, without waiting for gas to reach your engine.

h. Some players think that, since they can go their fastest in fourth gear, they should shift up to fourth as quickly as possible. What they fail to take into account, however, is that the car may not be ready to move into fourth so quickly, and the engine will lug, causing costly delays.

Although most of each race is spent in fourth, you should spend at least 2 seconds in the lower three gears first. The 2–3 seconds before moving into fourth allow the most innovation and creativity; they also present the greatest room for mistakes. This section of the race is by far the most important, since the player has fewer choices for optimum performance in fourth, giving him fewer decisions to make.

i. Try to keep the GAS button down from beginning to end, maintaining maximum safe torque. You may find it necessary to lift the button just before the finish if you are sure the engine is about to blow; if you only think it might blow, take the chance of keeping the button down. When going after records, you must take risks.

One way to gain a realistic idea of the risk you are taking with the button down is to watch your car's front wheels. You know exactly how close to the right edge they must come to finish the race. If the engine is screaming from pressure and you are not just about to finish, it may be wiser to release the button.

j. The current world record in DRAGSTER is 5.57 seconds, scored first by both Tony Armstrong of Cincinnati and Todd Rogers of Bridgeview, Illinois. Chuck Hunter, Sr., and Chuck Hunter, Jr., of Enon, Ohio, were the previous record holders with 5.61, just one-thirtieth of a second above. All four players, having experimented until they found the racing techniques best for them, know the game well. As an illustration of how widely successful methods may differ, here are summaries of three racing styles: Tony's, Todd's and the Hunters.'

Tony spends only about a quarter-second in first gear and twice that in second. In third, he watches the tach and shifts at the danger point, usually just over a second later. Once in fourth, he pops the clutch many times, but very lightly. He does not release the GAS button from beginning to end.

Todd spends about half a second in first gear, one and a half in second, and the same in third. He pops the clutch five or six times in fourth; interestingly, he releases the GAS button for a second each time, the only champion to do so.

Chuck Hunter and his elder son have scored 5.61 313 times between them. They start their typical race by shifting straight through first to second. They let the tach rise just to the beginning of the red zone before switching into third, where they stay for just under a second before proceeding to fourth. Once there, they do six low wheelies, two very quickly and the next four evenly spaced. They release the GAS button for an instant just before the end of the race, then finish with it down.

As different as the three winning techniques are, the record holders all stress the importance of practice. For every good race, even the best players must endure 50 or 60 failures. Still, even if you play at the leisurely pace of one race every 20 seconds, that means a good run about every 20 minutes, more than most other games promise.

k. If you find it difficult to distinguish the two cars' engine noises when playing doubles, use just your eyes to keep track of the tach, even turning the sound down all the way if you and your friend agree. You must know the game very well either to be able to distinguish your car's noises from his or to be able to drive without sound at all, and the variation is very good training. You may damage your basic game, however, if you play too much of Game 2, because it necessitates pushing the joystick in two more directions.

FREEWAY

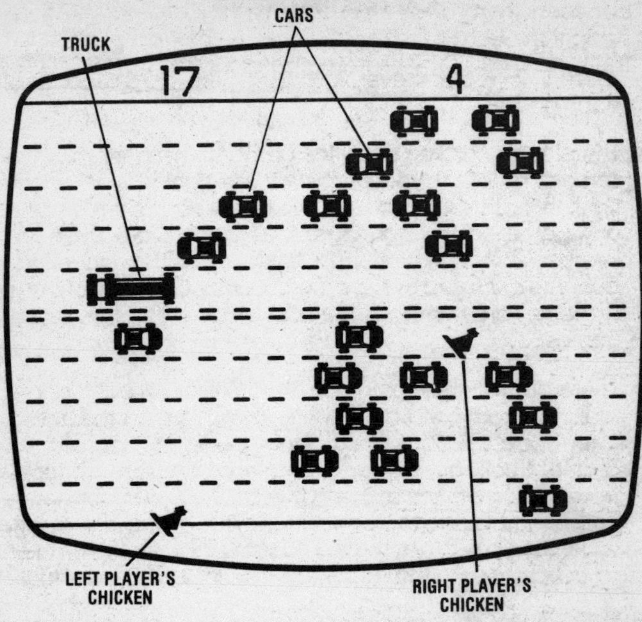

CONTROLS

a. Up-down joystick

SCORING

a. Each time the player's chicken reaches the top of the screen, the player scores a point.

DANGERS

a. The player's chicken is knocked back down the screen by every car or truck it touches.

b. The game ends after 2 minutes and 16 seconds.

OBSERVATIONS

a. The screen contains no clock or other time display. The two players' scores, however, flash during the last 8 seconds of each game.

b. The player's chicken starts the game at the bottom of the screen; the left player's on the left, the right player's on the right. As in DRAGSTER, one or two players can participate in any game on the cartridge. Their actions are even less interactive than in DRAGSTER, because neither player can become confused by the other's sounds. Observations and strategies are therefore identical for one- and two-player games.

c. There are 10 lanes for the chicken to cross in each game. Making it from one side of the freeway to the other therefore requires 11 steps. The bottom five lanes contain cars and/or trucks driving from left to right; the top five lanes, from right to left. The space between the two middle lanes, consisting of a dotted double yellow line, appears slightly wider than any other. There is no safe place for the chicken to stand, though, from top to bottom, including the middle.

d. The player's chicken moves up and down at his command but never sideways. In a way, the goal of the game is to be moving up as much of the time as possible. Standing still does not add to the total upward-moving time, but moving or being knocked backward subtracts from it. Whenever the chicken reaches the top of the screen, the player receives a point, and the chicken starts over immediately at the bottom.

e. When the chicken is hit, the car or truck does not stop for a moment. If the player's difficulty switch is set at a, the chicken is knocked back to the bottom of the screen; if it is set at b, it is knocked back only one and one-third lanes. If the chicken is hit in the head in difficulty b with the dividing line at its neck, it is knocked back so far that no part of it extends into the lane its body previously occupied.

Difficulty **b** is the standard. No matter how far back the chicken is knocked, there is always a slight pause before it can move again in either direction. During that pause, nothing protects it from being hit again.

f. In Game 1, the five top lanes' vehicles run symmetrically to those in the bottom lanes, although in the opposite direction. In the first three games, the lanes nearer the center have faster vehicles; from the drivers' perspective, those are the left lanes.

Game 1's vehicles are all single cars; that is, no lane has more than one car in it. As in every other game on the cartridge, any vehicle disappearing off one side emerges immediately from the other. The cars in Game 1's two center lanes travel five times as quickly as those in the two outside lanes, but they all travel so slowly that that difference means little.

g. Game 2, on the other hand, is asymmetrical. The fastest left-moving lane travels four times as fast as the slowest, but the ratio in the bottom of the screen is eight to one. The traffic consists of one truck, some single cars, some groups of cars close together (in effect, a truck), and some groups reasonably spread out. (The spaces are far enough, their speeds slow enough, that it is possible for a quick chicken to dart between two cars into the next lane.)

h. Game 3 has approximately the same type of traffic. There are no groups of cars without spaces, and the groups with spaces are traveling faster than in Game 2, making identical spaces seem slightly shorter. The lane-speed relationships are exactly the same on the top of the screen as on the bottom.

i. Game 4 features only ten vehicles, all fast-moving trucks. In each group of five lanes, this is how the speeds are related: the middle lane is the slowest, the two on either side are twice as fast, and the top and bottom are four times as fast.

j. Because every vehicle in the first four games moves at a contrast rate even after striking chickens, certain patterns emerge. In Game 2, for example, the traffic runs in cycles of approximately 30 seconds; in other words, all configurations repeeat themselves about every 30 seconds, or with every three crossings of the yellow car in the screen's bottom lane. Game 3's configurations repeat themselves at the same intervals; the three yellow cars in the bottom lane travel at the same rate as the one in Game 2, so they also cross the screen three times per cycle.

In Game 4, each cycle lasts only about 5 seconds; there are exactly 25⅔ cycles in each game. The reason for the shorter cycles is that the fast trucks cross the screen exactly four times, and the medium-speed ones exactly twice, in the time it takes the slowest trucks to cross once. Game 4 is also the only one with important sound effects; the player hears a zooming sound whenever a fast truck crosses, so there are exactly four zooms per cycle.

Games 5 through 8 have exactly the same traffic as Games 1 through 4, respectively, but the vehicles accelerate and decelerate randomly, preventing any pattern from forming.

STRATEGIES

a. After you select one of the first four games, just watch the traffic movement for a while without using your chicken. With no maneuvering to distract you, you can learn better and more quickly the patterns to be exploited. Once you are satisfied that you know what to do, you can start the game for real.

b. Whatever side of the screen your chicken is crossing, the traffic approaching from the near edge will be somewhat harder to avoid than that from the opposite side. If you use your peripheral vision to keep track of cars that disappear off the opposite edge, though, you should have a pretty good idea of when they will emerge next to you and of how fast they will be moving.

c. When you are about to start between two cars in the next lane, be sure that the lane beyond that is clear. It would be a shame to pull a masterly move only to find your hardy fowl knocked back by an unforseen spoilsport. To time your moves properly, you must plan well ahead.

d. Being hit is terrible for the serious player even with the difficulty switch set at **b.** Not only is the chicken lowered more than one lane, but also it stands still for about half a second after that, wasting precious time and risking being hit again. In difficulty **a**, of course, collision is a disaster. Do whatever you can, therefore, to prevent it. Even if you find that you must voluntarily move back down to avoid being hit, accept the escape route. Unless you have expertise to match them, forgo tight squeezes and oppressive risks.

e. When the unspeakable occurs and you are hit, consider your situation before presetting the joystick to shift your chicken up or down the instant it regains mobility. With the difficulty switch set at **b**, you must usually devote all your attention to escaping a second collision.

f. When playing against an opponent, ignore his score and collision noises. Observing them cannot tell you anything useful, and it may ruin your concentration.

g. In Game 1, the cars move so slowly that you should have no trouble in evading them. For the next three games, however, you need some kind of method to make mastery quicker and easier. The solution: learn Games 2, 3, and 4 in cycles.

Instead of learning the best possible way to survive in a patterned environment for 2 minutes and 16 seconds, you can devote all your energy to conquering a 5- or 30-second cycle, then repeat your winning technique over and over until the game ends.

Game 3 is harder to learn than Game 2; although their cycles are the same length, Game 3's more challenging traffic makes learning the perfect technique tricker. Game 4, with its 5-second cycles, is extremely easy to master, but the player is limited to 25 points per game. He needs less effort to achieve a lower potential.

h. In Games 5 through 8, there is no predicting where the next hit-and-run driver will emerge, so you must rely much more on timing and reflex than on strategy.

i. Ignore the traffic noises in every game but Game 4, for they are usually only for atmosphere and background. In Game

4, though, the zooms should help instill a sense of rhythm. Soon you may think of each cycle as lasting four zooms instead of one long crossing. Your ears can be useful, and peripheral vision may be inexact. In FREEWAY, you need precision. Why does the chicken cross the road? Because it's fun.

KABOOM!

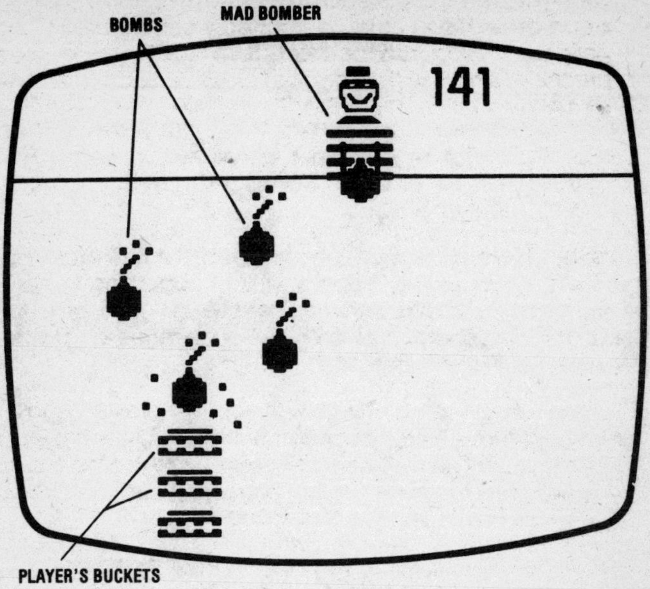

CONTROLS

a. Left-right dial

b. START button

SCORING

a. Bomb: 1–8 points

b. Bonus bucket every 1,000 points, with the player's buckets never exceeding three

DANGERS

a. If the player permits any bomb to reach the bottom of the screen, he loses a bucket.

b. The game ends when the player runs out of buckets.

OBSERVATIONS

a. The player starts each game controlling a stock of three wide, water-filled buckets, which he can move quickly along the botton of the screen with his dial. When his difficulty switch is set at **a**, his buckets retain their height but shrink to half their width.

b. The Mad Bomber moves along the top of the wall, dropping bombs. He may drop a bomb without appearing to stop, and there are also times when he reverses direction without dropping one, a more common occurrence later in the game. He is usually frowning.

c. Bombs always drop straight down. The player usually catches them in his top bucket; the ones he misses may fall into the second or third bucket if he is quick. A bomb, when caught, gives the player points, producing also an attractive splash in the graphics and sound effects.

When any bomb gets by the buckets and hits the bottom, all the bombs on the screen explode from bottom to top, the bomber smiles diabolically, and the player's lowest bucket vanishes.

d. There are eight groups of bombs, distinguished by the speed of descent, the number of bombs on the screen at a time, the value of each bomb, and the number of bombs in each group. Each bomb has a value the same as its group number. Group 1, for instance, with 10 bombs is worth 10 points in all. Group 2 has 20 bombs; Group 3, 30; Group 4, 40; Group 5, 50; Group 6, 75; Group 7, 100; and Group 8, 150.

The bombs fall at one of four speeds–Groups 1 and 2 the slowest, Groups 7 and 8 the fastest. The even-numbered screens may be considered harder, however, because they allow twice as many bombs on the screen at once. The odd-numbered groups feature 3, 4, 5, and 6 simultaneous bombs, respectively, as compared to 6, 8, 10, and 10–13 for the even-numbered groups. The player therefore has more bombs threatening to explode at any moment in an even-numbered group. The even-numbered groups' bombs, however, do fall in relatively predictable zigzag patterns.

e. The game starts with Group 1. Whenever the player completes a group successfully, pressing START will begin the next group. The first bomb falls where the last bomb of the last group did. As the group number rises, so does the splashing tone each bomb makes as it falls into a bucket.

When the player misses a bomb, he starts over one bucket poorer on the next group down. The group is the same in every way as the last time he faced it, except that it contains only half the bombs. Once he catches all those bombs, the player proceeds to the group in which he originally failed, hopefully having better luck this time.

f. If the player has three buckets already when passing a 1,000-point mark, he receives no bonus bucket. Even if he then loses one or more of his three, he must earn another 1,000 points for a chance at the bonus. Since the player keeps not his lowest but his highest bucket until last, catching bombs becomes much harder.

g. The longer a game lasts, the more it tests the player's stamina and eyes. Playing a sustained game requires precise, unflagging coordination.

h. When the player reaches 10,000 points, the bomber's mouth opens into an "O" to show his rage and astonishment. The bombs are almost exclusively in Groups 7 and 8 after 2,000 points, but the game gets harder even within Group 8. The bomber accelerates his horizontal motion gradually during the first 500,000 points or so, after which it levels off.

At certain times, such as 10,000 and 160,000, the bomber starts doing much more moving than bombing. His erratic, patternless course may lead him to drop 30 bombs on one side of the screen, then 30 on the other. His unpredictability at such times may lead the player on wild goose chases, causing him to miss bombs.

The player's maximum score is 999,999, shown without commas. The six digits do not turn to exclamation points as they do when a LASER BLAST player scores 1,000,000.

STRATEGIES

a. KABOOM! requires prodigious reflexes, but you will find it less strenuous the more you practice and the better you know the groups' patterns. Group 7 may actually be the hardest of all: although there are only six bombs on at a time, they fall very swiftly and are spread out unpredictably across the screen. Group 8 at least allows the player's bucket to move across the screen in a smooth, relatively regular back-and-forth sweep.

b. To do well at the game, you must be as confident with one bucket as with three. Otherwise, losing one bucket far from the next 1,000 mark may threaten your concentration, and losing two buckets more or less destroys your game. With practice, it doesn't have to be that way.

c. Once the bombs start falling really fast, you cannot focus on all of them. Either watch the bombs near the screen's edges and scan the center with peripheral vision, or watch the bomber and do your best to follow him step for step; since you reach each spot a fraction of a second later, you should catch every bomb he drops. As difficult as the latter method sounds, it is flawless when perfected. Mike Smithson of Grand Island, Nebraska, has used the technique to score 999,999 points, the maximum.

d. In the early part of each game, you can give yourself a rest and some extra points by letting a bomb go deliberately. Example: say your score is 550 and you have just completed five groups. If you go through Group 6 without missing, you will reach 1,000 points, losing your first opportunity for a bonus bucket. If you drop the group's last bomb, however, you will end up with 994 points and two buckets. You will recover your third immediately; by the time you repeat half of Group 5 and all of Group 6, though, you will have 1,569 points without having to brave Group 7. Later in the game, of course, this trick loses its usefulness.

e. Play with the difficulty switch set at **a** if you like, but it may disrupt your regular game. The variation is fun but unproductive.

f. Know the game's progression. You may find yourself hitting certain plateaus you will overcome with enough skill and practice. Especially common are plateaus at 1,000, 2,000, 10,000, and 100,000 points.

Rest between groups just to give your hands and eyes relief. If you stay away too long, though, you may lose your rhythmic sense and, when you start again, see your buckets go in quick succession. Another method of taking breaks is to play doubles, switching off at the controls with a friend. If either of you plays too long at a stretch, however, the other may get rusty. KABOOM! never lessens its demands.

LASER BLAST

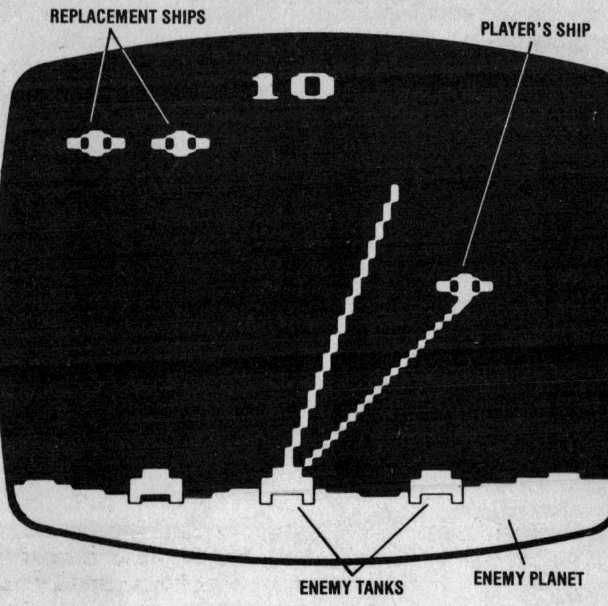

CONTROLS

a. Eight-directional joystick

b. AIM button

SCORING

a. Enemy tank: 10–90 points

b. Bonus ship every 1,000 points, never exceeding six.

DANGERS

a. If the player's ship is hit by any enemy laser beam, the ship is destroyed.

b. When the player runs out of ships, the game ends.

OBSERVATIONS

a. The player's ship starts the game at top left. Using the joystick, he can move it vertically, horizontally, and diagonally. When he is pressing AIM, however, he cannot maneuver his ship. Instead, a laser nozzle extends from the bottom of the ship, and he can use his joystick to direct the nozzle straight down, slightly to the left, or slightly to the right.

Whichever direction the nozzle is pointed, it fires a red laser beam the instant the player releases the AIM button. After shooting, the ship can either aim again or resume maneuvering.

b. The enemy tanks appear in screens of three. The tanks can both maneuver and fire, always staying the same distance apart. They all roll along the enemy planet's terrain in unison until one of them is directly beneath the player's ship. If the player's ship then moves, the tanks immediately start following it.

c. Periodically, one of the tanks extends a laser nozzle, aims it at the player's ship, and fires. If the player's ship manages to move out of the line of fire after the tank has aimed, it survives the blue flash; otherwise, it is hit.

Each tank can aim in several directions, none very far from straight up. Its aiming limitations are one reason it is programmed to move under the player's ship whenever possible. Its aiming and maneuvering are independent of each other, and it can do both at the same time.

The first tank to fire is usually but not always the middle one. After the first shot, the three take turns, always from left to right.

d. When the player's ship is hit, it turns pale blue and falls slowly to the ground. It can no longer aim, fire, or control its vertical movement, but it can control where it lands by maneuvering horizontally. A falling ship, if it lands on an enemy tank, will destroy that tank, earning the player points. Once the ship crashes, the player's replacement starts at top left.

e. LASER BLAST offers the player no opportunities for breaks.

As soon as he destroys the last tank of a screen, the next section of terrain scrolls on from the right, showing three more tanks.

The ship can maneuver freely in the meantime; if it chooses not to move, it starts the new screen in exactly the same position in which it finished the last. Each section of terrain is as wide as the picture tube.

The player cannot aim or fire, however, until the three tanks have reached center. They then immediately start rolling toward him unless he is over one of them already. After a brief pause, they also start shooting. The new screen has started.

f. Each screen of tanks has its own difficulty level, calculated by multiplying their relative ground speed and firing frequency. In Level 1, for example, the tanks roll slowly and have one shot on the screen every 2 seconds. In Level 2, they can roll twice as fast; in Level 4, they shoot once per second; in Level 8, they roll four times as fast; in Level 16, they fire twice per second; and in Level 32, the highest of the six, they can move along the planet surface eight times as fast. The more difficult a screen, moreover, the faster it scrolls into view.

How difficult screens become in the course of the game depends on the player's choice of game number. In Game 1, the screens never pass Level 8; Level 16 is the limit in Game 2. In Game 3, the screens gradually reach Level 32 but, in Game 4, the difficulty level jumps from 1 in the first screen to 32 in the second, where it stays.

g. In the first screen of any game, the player can move anywhere in the top half of the screen, prevented from descending farther by the enemy tanks' forçefield. Screen by screen, the forcefield moves up; by the time the player faces his ninth enemy trio, he can move only in a narrow space along the top of the screen, basically only horizontally.

The game becomes harder not just because the player's mobility is limited in general, but also because he is pushed up into the atmosphere. The lower the ship is flying, the shorter the horizontal distances it must fly to dodge its enemies' laser beams. When his ship is at the top of the screen, therefore, the player must remain at his most alert.

Some of the early LASER BLAST cartridges contained a minor bug: the player could stay below the rising forcefield by never releasing his AIM button except to fire. The ship never moved in any direction, including up. The flaw was not really important, since the method was difficult to master and affected only the player's first ship. Activision quickly eliminated it in later releases.

h. Along with the forcefields, the tanks' values rise in the first nine screens from 10 to 90, where they remain. The player receives a bonus ship every 1,000 points, although he can never have more than six replacements in stock at a time. As long as he loses no more than one ship every four screens, he can play indefinitely. The maximum possible score is 1,000,000; whenever the player's score exceeds 999,990, all six digits turn to exclamation points, and the game ends.

STRATEGIES

a. Learn LASER BLAST starting with Game 1, acquiring a solid familiarity with the maneuvering and firing habits of your ships and of the enemy tanks.

b. Keep your ship moving during battle. If you leave it in one place for a fraction of a second too long, one of the tanks is bound to draw a bead on it and fire.

Moving around is not all there is to survival, of course. You must move in sync with the game's rhythm, knowing exactly when an enemy is about to fire. One reason is that you cannot fly indefinitely in any direction. Evasive action, therefore, requires frequent reverses, and you do not want to reverse at the wrong moment. If you are not careful, you may fly straight into a tank's line of fire; it aims on your way over and fires on your way back. If you learn when to expect enemy lasers, you will know when not to reverse.

There are also times when you must stand still, when you

are aiming and firing. Ideally, you should be flying whenever the tanks are aiming and aiming whenever they are not. The difference is that you are shooting accurately, whereas they miss every time.

c. You should watch closely both your own ship and the tanks. With practice, your peripheral vision should tell you where your ship is, and your sense of rhythm will let you know when and where the tanks are firing.

d. Let the enemy fire the first shot of each screen. Until a tank has fired, keep moving evasively; once it has, you know when to expect each following shot and which tank will be firing it. This foreknowledge permits you to aim and fire at just the right moment, rather than receive any nasty surprises.

e. If your ship is unlucky enough to get hit, its usefulness is not quite ended. Steer it laterally so that it crashes onto a tank, earning points and countering a potential threat to your next ship.

f. Once you have picked a game number, know exactly how the screens increase their difficulty, revising your tactics accordingly. I consider Game 4 easier than Game 3, since you need adjust your sense of timing only once. In Game 3, the climb to Level 32 is so gradual that you must adopt several different tempos on the way, and later play is just as hard as in Game 4.

It is also easier to reach 1,000,000 points in Game 4 than in any other version, simply because it takes less time. Each Level 32 screen takes slightly under 2½ seconds. Since you must complete just over 3,700 screens, one game should take only about 2½ hours. Game 1, on the other hand, can take over 5 hours to complete, says David Crane, the game's designer. The fewer ships you lose, obviously, the faster you can reach 1,000,000 in any version.

g. LASER BLAST allows for several winning methods, but one is the most efficient. Start each screen at top left, moving to the right until the first tank fires and misses.

You should now be over the left tank. Fire straight down.

Then move slightly to the right, avoiding the next tank's shot. The tanks roll so quickly in Level 32 that you have to move only about half the distance to the middle tank, letting it meet you halfway. Fire straight down at it, repeat the process with the last tank, then zoom back to the left edge in preparation for the next screen.

h. If you have one of the early LASER BLAST cartridges, you can perhaps postpone being forced into the upper atmosphere for a few screens. If you are skilled enough, however, this elaborate technique is not worth the time or trouble. In general, in fact, there is nothing wrong with playing the whole game from the top of the screen. If you have the rhythm, the height shouldn't bother you.

i. If you are planning to try for 1,000,000 on, you must be properly prepared. Unlike ASTROSMASH, this game features no PAUSE key, so endurance becomes an important factor.

   Build up to the effort incrementally as in training for a marathon; if you have never reached 500,000, you will certainly have trouble with 1,000,000. If you feel you are ready to try, though, set aside enough time for the endeavor. Being interrupted by a telephone, for instance, is enough to end the game prematurely.

STAMPEDE

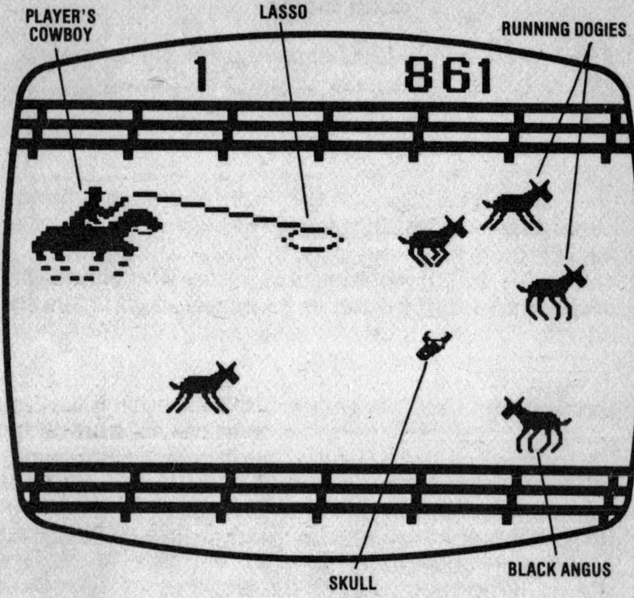

CONTROLS

a. Up-down joystick

b. THROW button

SCORING

a. Hereford: 3 points

b. Guernsey: 15 points

c. Jersey: 25 points

d. Angus: 100 points

e. Extra stray allowed every 1,000 points, never exceeding nine.

DANGERS

a. If the players' cowboy touches an Angus or the horse's feet touch a skull, the horse rears, delaying the player.

b. If the player lets too many dogies stray off the left edge of the screen, the game ends.

OBSERVATIONS

a. The player's cowboy gallops along a scrolling, fenced-in corral. He never actually moves horizontally, but the fences above and below him zip by from right to left, giving the illusion that he is galloping to the left.

Even though the cowboy's horse is always almost touching the screen's left edge, the player can use the joystick to shift him vertically. As long as the player pushes the joystick forward, the cowboy and his galloping horse move upward fairly slowly until they reach the top fence. The cowboy is free to maneuver vertically except when he is throwing his lasso or his horse is rearing.

b. When the player presses THROW, the loop of the lasso sails out in front of the cowboy. If it reaches its full length, the lasso reaches a spot directly in front of the cowboy's horse, then quickly coils again, returning to his hand. With the difficulty switch set at **a**, the rope extends about two lengths in front of the horse; with the switch set at **b**, it extends about two and a half lengths.

If the loop touches any dogie, though, the dogie disappears, and the lasso immediately rewinds. If a dogie is ahead of the cowboy but far within the lasso's range, he can rope it high and short. Instead of lasting its ordinary time of about a second, the throw then takes less time to complete.

If the player keeps the THROW button down, the loop automatically goes out again the instant it returns. The drawback, of course, is that the cowboy then cannot maneuver for twice as long. Once the lasso is thrown, nothing can halt the toss until the loop hits a dogie or the end of its range and then returns.

c. The points earned by roping dogies are added to the score display one by one, but quickly. If the player has a score like 2,910, for example, then ropes an Angus but lets his last allowable stray go by, the game will end regardless of the bonus allowable stray the player had already earned by topping 3,000. The computer's decisions are always based on the score displayed at that moment, ignoring whatever points the player has coming to him.

The player starts the game with only three allowable strays. If he lets three dogies go off the left edge before reaching 1,000, the game ends. He earns an extra allowable stray every 1,000 points; since he can never have more than nine, however, he will not receive one at 7,000 if he has had a perfect record so far.

d. The corral actually comprises six lanes in which the dogies may appear. Except for Anguses, all dogies run to the right, none quite so swiftly as the player's horse. Herefords are the fastest and darkest runners, Guernseys are medium in both color and speed, and Jerseys are the slowest and the lightest. The slower a dogie, the more trouble it gives the player: it is overtaken by the player's horse sooner, thus threatening to stray sooner after emerging from the screen's right edge.

e. If a running dogie is close to the screen's left edge, the player can either rope it or herd it. To be herded, the dogie must touch any part of the cowboy, his horse, or the lasso if it is not being thrown. Once contact occurs, the dogie uses a burst of speed to reach the right edge again, where it resumes running at its usual pace.

Dogies sometimes run single file in groups of two or three. Even once the back dogie of a group has slipped behind the horse's back hoofs, it is not necessarily lost until it actually vanishes off the screen. If the cowboy manages to touch the next dogie in the group, the whole group scurries to the right. Moreover, whenever a group of dogies is herded, they do not resume normal speed until the back dogie reaches the screen's right edge.

Unfortunately, no dogie can be herded an infinite number of times. On its fourth herding, a dogie starts getting stubborn, resuming its normal pace a sixteenth of the way from the right edge. If the player persists in herding it, the dogie slows down again after crossing only seven-eighths of the screen, then three-quarters, then five-eighths, then half, then three-eighths, then a quarter, until herding has no effect on the dogie at all.

f. Anguses do not run and cannot be herded. They are black and stand still in their lanes, facing defiantly left. They can be roped by an alert player but, if he tries to herd them, his horse rears. Not only does he lose time, but the Angus gets by him, counting as a stray.

g. Sun-bleached skulls make the horse rear if its feet touch them, and the skulls cannot even be roped. The player does not need to rope them, of course, since he is not penalized for letting them go off the left edge.

h. In Game 1 of STAMPEDE, everything emerging from the screen's right edge does so in a complicated but logical pattern. Every lane's dogies appear in regular cycles of Jersey-Guernsey-Hereford-skull or Jersey-Guernsey-Hereford-Angus. Except for the skull or Angus at the end, a group of Jerseys will always be followed by groups of the other dogies identical in number and spacing. Example: two Jerseys close together are always followed in the same lane by two Guernseys close together, then by two Herefords close together, then by an Angus or a skull, then by more Jerseys, and so forth.

In any given lane, there can never be dogies of different colors on the screen at a time. An entire group must stray or be roped, preferably the latter, before the lane's next group can appear. The horses in each cycle always appear at the same intervals; that is, if the player ropes two identical groups in neighboring lanes one right after the other, the next groups will be the same in both lanes and will appear one right after the other.

i. It may seem that there is no way of predicting whether an Angus or a skull will appear after the last Hereford in a lane strays or is roped. Actually, the corral's hazards appear quite predictably. They alternate. The first hazard to appear in every game is a skull; the second, a bull, and so on.

The pattern is not always easy to follow, of course. When a player ropes two groups of Herefords in a short period, for example, he can expect one skull and one Angus any second. To know which will be in which lane, though, he must remember two things:

1. Whether the last hazard to appear was a skull or an Angus

2. The order in which he cleared the two lanes of Herefords

If the last hazard was an Angus, for instance, and he roped all the Herefords in the top lane first, then the top lane will give him a skull while the lower one supplies an Angus.

One last complexity: there is an exception to the above rule, one rare situation in which the top lane would contain the Angus. If the top lane's Herefords were actually farther from the cowboy when he roped them than the bottom lane's and if he then roped the bottom lane's **without herding them,** the bottom lane's Herefords count as the first ones roped, and so the skull appears not in the top but in the bottom. Such a circumstance is extremely uncommon, though, and occurs usually early in the game and with single Herefords roped.

j. In every lane, each cycle is slightly different from the last, and the cycles appear in identical order in every lane. The first cycle in each lane contains one dogie of each color; the second, two dogies close together; the third, two somewhat separated; the fourth, three close together; the fifth, two quite far apart; the sixth, three somewhat separated; the seventh, one; the eighth, two close together, and so on.

As the game progresses, the groups and cycles in each lane spread out just as the individual dogies do, making each appearance somewhat harder to anticipate. Furthermore, In Games 1 through 4, the dogies accelerate from a slow trot to a brisk gallop. Their speeding up does not matter so much, but the cowboy's horse does the same, making everything in the corral happen the same way but faster. The only part of the game that stays slow is the cowboy's vertical maneuvering speed.

The score display can show no more than four figures. Every time the player reaches 10,000 points, no mean feat, a coded symbol resembling a steer's head appears at the bottom left.

k. The player can choose several variations to make the 'game harder. In Game 3, for example, the dogies and skulls all appear randomly, preventing him from predicting any opportunities or dangers.

Games 2 and 4 are identical to Games 1 and 3, respectively, except that the dogies do not run straight across the screen. They all shift slightly in a rhythmic up-and-down motion, but no dogie can pass the boundaries of its lane.

Games 5 through 8 are like Games 1 through 4 except that the dogies start out at full gallop rather than accelerate gradually. Past a certain point, of course, the second set of four is no more difficult than the first.

STRATEGIES

a. Learn to judge your maneuvering speed accurately. If a dogie is too far away and too far to the left to herd before it strays, know when to give up on it. Chasing it futilely will do nothing but waste precious time, possibly permitting another dogie to slip by.

b. Know when and when not to be pressing the THROW button. If you keep it down too much, its usefulness decreases because there is no lane with a constant supply of dogies. Often, when only one throw is necessary, beginners keep the button down an instant too long, sending the loop out again. When several different dogies are threatening to stray–and they certainly do as the game progresses–you do not want to have to stand still for an extra second.

Furthermore, when you want to rope only the back dogie or two of a group, keeping the button down a fraction of a second longer than necessary will not only waste your time but also rope the last of the group, letting the next group on when you wanted to delay it. (See Strategy h.)

Especially easy to misjudge is the time you need for a short throw. The loop comes back so quickly that you may well have the button still down, losing what may be a crucial second of mobility. When you need only one throw, press the button quickly and release.

c. When an Angus appears, you want to switch to his lane and rope him. Only if you know you have no chance of roping him should you stay away, giving your horse no chance to rear. Still, you can usually rope even Anguses with high, short throws. Skulls, on the other hand, are undesirable in any case, so stay away from them.

d. In Game 1, know the dogie cycles and their progression by heart. Otherwise, you might as well be playing Game 3. Keep track of what stage in its cycle each of the six lanes has reached.

e. When the dogies follow a pattern, as they do in Game 1, you know enough about home video by now to be aware that you can devise an optimum pattern for yourself. When you have done so, it is usually wise to stick to the pattern from the beginning, ensuring that everything occurs in a predictable way.

f. When the last Hereford of a group somehow strays, don't just think, That's too bad. An Angus may well appear any second, so be prepared. If you have been following the pattern described below, you will let very few Herefords slip by; even when they do, you will know whether they will be followed by Anguses or skulls.

g. If herding Herefords did not eventually make them subborn, you could pick more or less any herding pattern and play indefinitely. You could herd Herefords in the bottom five lanes, for example, intermittently roping dogies as they appear in the top lane until you have completed an entire cycle. Then go through a cycle in the second lane, then in the third, until you have completed one cycle in every lane and can start a new cycle in the top lane. If you keep only one lane open at a time, you will never have to worry about any surprises.

This method actually works for 1,500 or so points, after which the pace becomes a little too fast. The problem is that it takes too long to complete a cycle. The player must keep herding any given group of Herefords while he runs through the cycle in the other five lanes. Although Herefords are the fastest dogies and therefore require the least herding, each group of them must be herded about 15 times in the one-open-lane technique before finally being roped. Ten would be too many. In fact, their stubbornness becomes a vicious circle. The stubborner they become, the more often the player must herd them. Sooner or later, the one-open-lane method must fail.

The player can cut the time per cycle by about half by keeping two lanes open at a time; first the top two, then the middle, then the bottom. He must then watch the open lanes more alertly, but he has fewer and less stubborn Herefords to herd in the meantime. This technique is most effective during the easy stretches in which dogies appear frequently.

The best method for cycles with dogies far apart scores points in the shortest time and requires the least herding. Keep the top three lanes open until you have completed a cycle in all three, then go to the bottom three and follow the same procedure. Each cycle can then be completed in two phases, as opposed to six or three. One would be impossible, of course.

h. Three open lanes are not too many for an experienced player to handle when the dogies appear infrequently. To begin with, try to open the three lanes (rope all the Jerseys, Guernseys, Herefords) as close to simultaneously as possible, permitting you to predict exactly when the next group in each lane will appear. You will then be able to rope all three groups in one smooth motion up or down.

When you are dealing with groups of two or three, it is usually worthwhile to clear the back dogie or two of each group before roping the front dogies and permitting the next groups on. That way, you can be sure that the next groups will appear one right after the other, and you can follow the same procedure with them until you have completed that cycle in all three lanes. As unimportant as this tactic appears, it can double or triple your final score.

Since you clear three groups of Herefords at a time, you must have a very clear idea of which lanes will then give you Anguses. Depending on whether the last hazard was an Angus or a skull, you are bound to receive either one or two skulls. Using the information in Observation **i**, you should be able to plan a successful Angus-roping, skull-avoiding course with just a little concentration.

Since you are covering three open lanes at once, you want to spend as little time as possible herding in the other three. Ideally, you should need only one trip up and back, or down and back, to herd all three Hereford groups. For your horse to touch all three groups in one journey, they must be quite close together horizontally. If you know how the pattern works, you can get them clustered by finishing off their predecessors as close to simultaneously as possible.

Still, even if you make a mistake, you can certainly take steps to bring three divergent groups into a cluster. Simply decide which group is too far to the left in each herding. Touch that group with your horse's back hoofs but herd the others with the tip of its nose. You will narrow the gap each time until you can herd all three groups without hesitating or making more than one trip, thus allowing yourself more time to deal with the three open lanes. Try it and see.

i. The lovely pattern above requires only a little practice to perfect. If you are playing with randomly appearing dogies, however, it does you no good, and you must simply cross your fingers, hoping to be in the right place at the right time. Unless you have exceptional luck, you will have trouble scoring over 3,000 points.

When the dogies start the game at full gallop, you must be ready for challenging action earlier than usual. The short lasso of difficulty **a** is a disadvantage because you will have less control of when to rope approaching dogies. Since you will have to wait longer to rope some dogies, you will have to spend more time herding the others. In the games that permit the dogies to wander up and down slightly, you must slip into their rhythm yourself to be sure that your throws are accurate. Snap out of the rhythm temporarily, however, whenever confronting skulls or Anguses; they remain menacingly still.

7

OFF-TELEVISION EXERCISES

Physical adeptness is essential to implementing your strategies. In your spare time, you and a friend can work on improving hand-eye coordination, peripheral vision, finger strength, and tempo control. The exercises, many of which received favorable reviews after appearing in **How To Master the Video Games,** are herein revised and augmented. They can be enjoyably challenging and sharpen skills effectively, but they should be adjusted to each player's abilities and needs.

Hands

You will accomplish wonders by training your hands to react as quickly as possible to visual stimuli.

Exercise: have your friend drop a pen from various heights, from as high as he can reach to shoulder level. Stand a foot away and keep your right hand at your side until you see the pen drop; then reach and catch it before it hits the ground. (See diagram.) Your hand should not rise to meet the pen but should catch it from the side, which requires precise timing. The different heights are necessary to prevent your relying more on reflex than on actual coordination. When you have made ten clean catches in a row with each hand, let your friend try.

Eyes

Some games use sound effects to warn the player of danger; a top-notch player, however, must also be alert to the slightest flicker of movement in any part of the screen and be able to analyze all visual data without shifting focus. This abilty is particularly important in such fast-moving challenges as KABOOM!

Exercise: have your friend stand 3 feet from you at about 2 o'clock. Stare straight ahead while he holds up a random number of fingers; call out how many you see. If you are correct on the first try, have your friend move more and more to your right side until you make a wrong guess. He should then maintain his position. Keeping your head **and** eyes straight ahead, try to concentrate enough to answer correctly five times in a row. Repeat the exercise on your left side; then switch with him.

This exercise is designed to strengthen your natural peripheral vision. Often, what you see "out of the corner of your eye" can mean life or death on screen.

Fingers

Anyone who has played games using button, dial, or disc controls knows how essential digital skill can be. Since sustained play produces pain and slowness in the joints of unprepared fingers, fingers must be strong and limber.

Thumbs are especially susceptible to overuse during play, so try to alternate as much as possible. If you feel your left thumb getting tired on the Atari, for instance, see how efficiently your left forefinger can take over. Try also to use the small joints in each finger much less than the larger one.

Before playing any of the games, it is best to do a few minutes of warm-up exercises for all ten fingers. Pull each one back as far as it will go and keep it there for 10 seconds, loosening and stretching the muscles that might otherwise cramp. For the Intellivision games, which require exceptional forefinger endurance, here is one effective way to warm up.

Exercise: wrap the fingers of your right hand tightly around a pen. Then extend the forefinger and begin to rotate it clockwise around a doorknob. You should start slowly, at about 30 revolutions per minute (rpm), retaining your grip on the pen and keeping your wrist as stationary as possible. Try never to touch the doorknob and never to wander more than half an inch from it.

Your finger should hurt slightly: the muscles are being loosened and limbered. Now accelerate the rotations to 60 rpm. If you can hold your orbit for 1 minute, you are doing well.

Now alternate between clockwise and counterclockwise motion, starting slowly and increasing speed each time. Finally, repeat the entire process with your left hand.

Tempo

Advanced play in all video games requires a firm command of timing; often, this mastery involves the ability to fall into various rhythms inherent to the games. Two examples are the move-stop-shoot rhythm so crucial in SPACE INVADERS and the UFO and guided-missile rhythms in ASTROSMASH.

Exercise: try to tap a pen on a table at intervals of **exactly** 1 second for 30 seconds, having a friend time you. Once you have accomplished that, move up to intervals of 2 seconds for a minute, then of 3 seconds for a minute and a half, and so on.

Intervals of 7 seconds are the most difficult you are likely to need for developing sufficient rhythmic skill.

When setting out to learn a game, you should always decide on the best way to hold and to use the controls. To protect your eyes, don't sit close to the TV set and play in the dark as seldom as possible. Find a playing posture that is easy on your neck, back, and shoulders, and don't forget to switch positions occasionally to prevent strain. Even when you are playing in the best type of position, erect but relaxed, you will probably not want to play for too long without resting and stretching. Games such as KABOOM! and ASTROSMASH offer ample opportunity for such beneficial interruptions.

The **New England Journal of Medicine** of May 28, 1981, reported a case of "SPACE INVADERS wrist" that could well have been avoided with proper preventive measures. Home video games are not boring even when played for hours, so do what you can to be sure that cramps and pains will not hinder your enjoyment or performance.

8

RECORDS AND CLUBS

RECORDS

ATARI

Most Atari games are unsuited for record breaking for two reasons: there are many variations in each cartridge, and records are hard to verify. Most Atari action games have score displays that "turn over" every so often, so at no point is there any proof of a really high score.

The two scores below, however, were attained during national tournaments, and they are the closest things to official records that Atari has.

ASTEROIDS: 138,670 points in Game 6, difficulty **a**–Douglas Pye of Belaire, Texas

SPACE INVADERS: 165,200 points in Game 1, difficulty **a**–Bill Heineman of Whittier, California

INTELLIVISION

ARMOR BATTLE, SEA BATTLE, and SPACE BATTLE are not games for record-scoring, and SPACE ARMADA has no official records yet. The fifth game in this book, however, does have a record holder:

ASTROSMASH: 862,780 points–Douglas Rochler of Huntington Station, New York

ACTIVISION

DRAGSTER: 5.57 seconds in singles–(1) Tony Armstrong of

Cincinnati, Ohio; (2) Greg Nichols of Hudson, Indiana; (3) Todd Rogers of Bridgeview, Illinois

5.64-second tie in doubles–Chuck Hunter and Chuck Hunter, Jr., of Enon, Ohio

FREEWAY: 34 points in Game 3–Russell DeWolfe of Arlington, Texas

KABOOM!: 999,999 points–(1) Alan Feinman of Richboro, Pennsylvania; (2) Jim Munsterman of Napa, California; (3) Joe O'Hara of Yuba City, California; (4) Brian and Jay Press of San Pedro, California; (5) Mike Smithson of Grand Island, Nebraska

LASER BLAST: First to score 1,000,000 points in 2½ hours–Janet Stuckey of Indianapolis, Indiana

STAMPEDE: 24,578 points–Ken Vance of Las Vegas, Nevada

CLUBS

Atari Game Club
P.O. Box AGC
Half Moon Bay, LA 94019 — Membership: $1.00

Intellivision Game Club
P.O. Box 4010
Burlingame, CA 94010 — Membership: $1.50

The Activision game clubs are open to all cartridge owners who send in proof of proficiency. Once you achieve the score required, simply take a picture of the screen and send it to: Jan Marsella; Activision, Inc; 3255-2 Scott Boulevard; Santa Clara, CA 95051

World Class Dragster Club: under 6 seconds

The Save the Chicken Foundation: 20 points in Game 3 or 7 of FREEWAY

The Activision Bucket Brigade: 3,000 points in KABOOM!

The Federation of Laser Blasters: 100,000 points on Game 3 or 4

The Activision Trail Drive: 3,000 points in STAMPEDE

9

COMING ATTRACTIONS: PAC-MAN AND OTHERS

Atari, the company that started the home video craze, has 12 new releases planned for 1982, bringing their catalogue of games into the high fifties. Their new cartridges include adaptations of several popular arcade games: BERZERK, DEFENDER, PAC-MAN, and SUPER BREAKOUT. PAC-MAN is due for release in March, but I was lucky enough to get a glimpse of an advance copy. For those Atarians who have cartridges by the time **How To Master Home Video Games** is released, here are 13 useful tips based on my advance viewing.

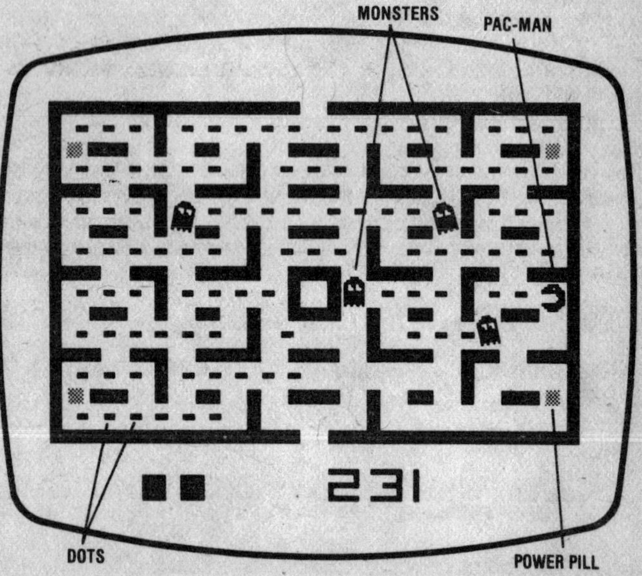

1. Know the structure of the PAC-MAN maze. The home version has 126 dots in each screen, as opposed to 240 in the arcade. (See Chapter 11.) The maze is horizontal, of course, instead of vertical, but there are still four Power Pills.

2. The player starts with four Pac-Men, only one of which is on the screen at a time. When a Pac-Man is touched by a monster, he is done for, and his replacement starts over near bottom center.

   Learn to use the joystick correctly. You will find that constant pressure is not needed to keep the Pac-Man moving. You can set him on a course just by tapping in one of four directions, and he will keep going until he hits a wall. You will control him better with a light touch than with a heavy one.

3. Turns tend to slow many players down, so keep your Pac-Man on the long straightaways when you can. If you must turn, it helps to preset the joystick before reaching the intersection. That way, he can take the turn as quickly as a monster.

   Do not be afraid to flee a monster while eating dots. Unlike his arcade counterpart, your Pac-Man can run just as swiftly while gobbling.

4. In the arcade, each monster's eyes indicate the direction in which he is moving or about to move. No such luck here, because the eyes are all rotating clockwise, not remaining in one position. If you know how the monsters are tracking you, though, you can predict their movements easily. The monsters appear white but are actually lightly shaded; the differences are more obvious in the black-and-white mode. Try it and see.

   When a monster is pursuing you and reaches an intersection, it chooses whatever route leads to you most directly. Monsters can never reverse, though, so they are easy to mislead. Simply lure one into committing itself at an intersection, then zip back, around, and out. In almost any situation, the maze gives you some escape route.

5. The more monsters are chasing you, the more challenging escaping becomes. Do your best to stay away from gangs, therefore, using your peripheral vision to keep track of every monster on the screen. If they seem to be closing in on you, escape. When learning this defense method, you may wish to have the monsters chase you at "walking" or "jogging" speed rather than "running." Pick your game number accordingly.

6. The monsters sometimes travel together, clustering two, three, or even four on top of one another. It may be hard to tell how many there are in such a cluster, and you don't want to be trapped by a monster that suddenly becomes two monsters. It really is necessary to watch the movements of every monster on the screen, enabling yourself to make strategic decisions without doubt or hesitation.

7. You can often escape monsters through the tunnel that connects top and bottom center. They rarely follow you through the tunnel; if you do see one go in after you, get away quickly from the tunnel's other end.

8. Power Pills give you temporary superiority over the monsters; chasing and eating them can earn you points. Try to clear the board of dots one quadrant at a time but leave the Power Pills for the latter part of each screen. Since the monsters will all be chasing you by then, they will be easier to gobble up after you eat each pill. Never let a pill be the last edible object on the screen, though, if you want it to be useful; the next screen starts as soon as you eat it, and you have no opportunity for chasing monsters. The last thing you eat in each screen should be a dot.

9. You must envelop the whole pill to eat it, not just half or three-quarters. It may be dangerous to wait until the last possible minute to eat a pill, for a monster may touch you before you have "digested" the pill completely.

10. The eyes of monsters you eat return to their lair at the screen's center, where the monsters rematerialize and then come out again. If you devour one right after the other, two or more may re-emerge as one monster, then split. After eating any number of monsters, be very careful

around their lair; a monster newly emerging can be deadly.

11. Two high-value vitamins appear directly under the lair during each screen. Once on, each lasts about 15 seconds before disappearing if left to itself. You cannot predict when each vitamin will appear, but do your best to snap it up once it does, earning at least 98 extra points (100 for the vitamin minus 2 for the two dots it replaced).

12. With the difficulty switch set at **a,** the monsters are edible for shorter periods, and the vitamins disappear sooner.

13. Do the monsters move in patterns? Definitely. The patterns are tough to crack, though, so make the attempt only if you are a serious player. Once you do figure them out with observation, experimentation, and memorization, you can devise your own pattern to score the maximum points in each screen, lasting through as many screens as possible. Even without patterns, though, with just these 12 strategies and practice, you can enjoy the home PAC-MAN and still score quite respectably.

Atari is also debuting a new game system this year, one with much greater memory potential and with improved graphics and sounds. (Even a voice synthesizer is promised.) The system will offer many interesting games, including such arcade favorites as SPACE INVADERS, PAC-MAN, and GALAXIAN.

Intellivision is working energetically to bring out interesting games. Team sports are one specialty, but recent action games have proved exciting with realistic graphics and sound effects. With an additional keyboard component, the system converts to a home computer.

Activision has been extremely successful in producing cartridges for the Atari system, and the two newest releases, BARNSTORMING and GRAND PRIX, conform to the company's standard of excellence. The Santa Clara manufacturer is no longer alone in producing just software, however. Makers such as Imagic newborn have announced intentions of producing cartridges for both the Atari and the Intellivision systems.

These are not the only two systems available, of course.

Magnavox's Odyssey is the third most popular system and is trying hard to move up. The Bally Professional Arcade, now produced by Astrovision, is very good but has a more limited ownership. Minor systems such as Fairchild's Channel F and the APF are also still in the picture; they run cheaper but offer less impressive collections of games.

The year 1982 will bring many impressive games, and designers will have more and more chances to show their diligence and creativity. The system owners will have amazing new game libraries from which to choose. I believe that home video is an industry whose time has come.

10

THE CASE OF THE PROUD PROGRAMMER

Home video games are so much fun that many players enjoy them happily without ever wondering what really goes on behind the cartridges. In the past ten years, though, the people behind the games have built not only an industry but also a community, one with its own flamboyant characters, its own legends and rumors. One of the more amusing oddities of recent home video history seems interesting enough to include in this volume.

Unlike Activision, Atari and Intellivision do not set forth written credit for their programmers for even the most imaginative work. The games are Atari's or Intellivision's, and that is all the consumer is told.

Warren Robinett, the designer of Atari's recent release ADVENTURE, was so eager for public acknowledgment that he staked a hidden claim in his own program. Most owners have played for hours without the slightest notion that it existed, but the "Programmer's Room" is worth seeing for those who know how to find it. (See diagram on page 182).

The cartridge, with its medieval supernatural setting, is in itself distinctive. The player controls an adventurer whose ultimate goal is to fetch an enchanted chalice from the Gray Dungeon of the Black Castle and bring it home to the Golden Castle. In Games 2 and 3 of ADVENTURE, which this chapter concerns, the kingdom is large enough to include a White Castle and several assorted rooms, labyrinths, dungeons, and catacombs (in which the player has visibility of only a few inches).

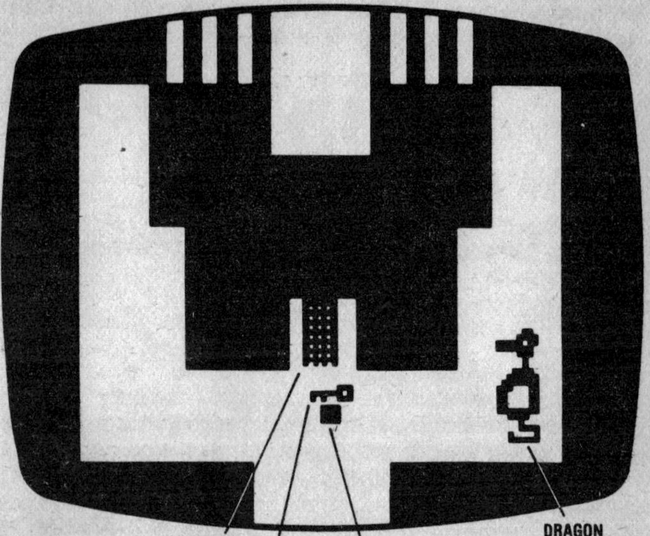

To assist him in his quest, the player has a sword for protection; a magnet to attract any inanimate objects in the same region of the kingdom; and a magical bridge to scale all catacomb and labyrinth walls. Unfortunately, he can carry only one object with him at a time; he must release it before he can pick up another.

Opposing him are Yorgle, Grundle, and Rhindle–yellow, green, and red dragons, respectively. They attempt to eat any adventurer bold enough to enter their domains, and they can be thwarted only with death by sword. A black bat also causes trouble by suddenly swapping objects with the adventurer, leaving him with useless things. If he can catch the bat, though, he can use it to carry and switch objects for him until it escapes or is released.

This is by no means a complete explanation of ADVENTURE, but I do want players to know how to find the "Programmer's Room" by themselves. It has nothing to do with winning the game; nevertheless, the phenomenon is intriguing. Here, then, for those with access to the cartridge, are step-by-step directions to the room almost no one has seen:

1. Select Game 2, with difficulty switch set at **b.**
2. Press RESET.
3. Move left to catch the bat, which is carrying the sword.
4. Leave the Golden Castle's vestibule and descend to the Great Corridor. Turn right and wait above the Catacombs for Grundle to appear.
5. He will emerge from the right edge of the screen. When he approaches you, run him through with the sword and leave the corpse there.
6. Descend with bat and sword into the Catacombs, where you can force the bat to exchange the sword for the Golden Key.
7. Return to the Golden Castle, using the key to unlock the gates. Once you have entered, release the bat and leave. You have imprisoned the bat in your castle, and it should not bother you again. Be careful not to re-enter the Golden Castle until you return with the Enchanted Chalice.
8. Return to the Great Corridor and turn left this time. Then make the first right, into the Blue Labyrinth.
9. Find your way through the Blue Labyrinth to the White Key.
10. Pick up the key and leave the Blue Labyrinth. Then travel the length of the Great Corridor until you can turn down into the Catacombs again.
11. Wend your way through the Catacombs down and to the left. When you emerge, take the first right and you will find yourself in the vestibule of the White Castle. Do not enter but drop the White Key there and leave.
12. Fetch the sword from the Catacombs. You will need it.
13. At last, use the White Key to enter the castle. Drop it then because Yorgle attacks almost immediately. Run to the

sword you have left in the vestibule. Once you recover it, skewer the dragon.

14. Leave the sword outside the castle; then go and fetch the Bridge from the Catacombs. You need it to enter a certain secret passage in the White Castle's Red Labyrinth.

15. Do so. Travel along the secret passage until you find the Black Key. Pick it up and retrace your steps. Cross the bridge and take the key from the White Castle.

16. You must now take the Black Key, the sword, and the Bridge to the Black Castle on the other side of the Blue Labyrinth. The quickest method is to use the Bridge to take short cuts through the Catacombs and the Blue Labyrinth, carrying the other two objects over it.

17. Once all three are near the gates of the Black Castle, enter with the Black Key. Leave it and bring in the sword.

18. With the sword, roam the Gray Dungeon until you encounter Rhindle. You will need skill and speed to vanquish him.

19. You now have no need for your sword. Any other player would pick up the Enchanted Chalice and happily bring it home, but you know better. Take the sword out and bring in the Bridge, ignoring the chalice.

20. Wander around with the Bridge until you find yourself in a part of the dungeon whose walls flash, although there are no other objects on the screen.

21. Mr. Robinett has placed a tiny secret room at the bottom of the screen, slightly left of center. Enter it with your Bridge.

22. The room may appear empty, but it is not. Sweep along the bottom wall until you hear that you have picked something up.

23. Leave by the Bridge. Pass through the Gray Dungeon, the Black Castle's gates, and the Blue Labyrinth into the Great Corridor. By now you can see what you are carrying; it is a tiny speck, the Transmolecular Dot. You will soon see why it is so named.

24. Go all the way to the corridor's right end, where you should find Grindle's corpse. Drop the dot in a safe place.

25. Go find any object–sword, bridge, key, magnet, chalice, whatever. Bring it to the right end of the corridor.

26. Drop it and pick up the Transmolecular Dot. Holding the dot ahead of you, you are ready to perform a seemingiy impossible feat.

27. Head right, through the line at the end of the corridor. Only under these circumstances can you pass through it but, once you have, you will be glad you took the trouble. Behold, in flashing letters, CREATED BY WARREN ROBINETT. He has earned immortality.

11

THE ARCADE CONNECTION

It is estimated that more than 30 million Americans have played coin-operated video games with the last year. The enthusiasts range from quick-fingered preteens to determined businessmen, from adventurous women to grizzled SPACE INVADERS veterans. Over 470,000 of the machines were sold in 1981, and manufacturers are anticipating an even better year in 1982.

Play Meter, a leading industry magazine, conducted a readers' poll to determine the 25 top video games of 1981. They obtained the following results:

1. DEFENDER (Williams Electronics, Inc.)
2. PAC-MAN (Midway Manufacturing Co.)
3. ASTEROIDS (Atari, Inc.)
4. CENTIPEDE (Atari)
5. SCRAMBLE (Stern Electronics, Inc.)
6. PHOENIX (Centuri, Inc.)
7. GORF (Midway)
8. GALAXIAN (Midway)
9. BERZERK (Stern)
10. ASTEROIDS DELUXE (Atari)
11. MONACO GP (Sega Enterprises, Inc.)

12. MISSILE COMMAND (Atari)

13. WIZARD OF WOR (Midway)

14. ASTRO BLASTER (Sega)

15. STAR CASTLE (Cinematronics, Inc.)

16. OMEGA RACE (Midway)

17. CRAZY CLIMBER (Nichibutsu USA Corp.)

18. ARMOR ATTACK (Cinematronics)

19. RALLY-X (Midway)

20. CARNIVAL (Sega)

21. BATTLEZONE (Atari)

22. VENTURE (Exidy, Inc.)

23. MOON CRESTA (Sega)

24. PLEIADES (Centuri)

25. SUPER COBRA (Stern)

Home video games are undeniably challenging and exciting, and their advocates point out several advantages over the coin-operated variety. In the first place, players can enjoy the home games in complete privacy and whenever they please but may be asked to leave machines in the arcade by others who want turns. Moreover, after the modest initial investment in console and cartridges, home games offer unlimited play, whereas the arcade machines swallow a quarter or more for a single game.

There is, however, another side to the story. Although home video technology is every bit as advanced as arcade video, the home video programmers have much less space in which to position circuits and memory chips. Their games cannot help but have somewhat less impressive graphics and sound effects. Considering the difference in cost and convenience, home video can be a fine bargain; arcade video, though, is still worth experiencing.

Arcades have recently begun calling themselves "family amusement centers" to counteract the disadvantage of an undeservedly poor public image. Another slight disadvantage of arcade video is that machine owners sometimes use so-called enhancement kits to speed up their games or make the programs more difficult. On the other hand, arcades can surround players with an enjoyably high-tech environment, and only there can a certain special type of camaraderie be found.

I think that arcade video games are fascinating. Here are quick overviews of last year's top ten. (For longer, more comprehensive explanations of 30 popular games, see **How To Master the Video Games.**)

Game 1: DEFENDER

DEFENDER is a very complicated game, but less so than its "sequel," this year's STARGATE. Even the earlier version confronts the player with no fewer than six different controls and six species of enemy. The screen shows a planet surface over which the player's ship can fly in both directions. His main goal, apart from scoring points, is to save the planet's humanoids from their would-be kidnappers, the landers. He must also avoid having his ship destroyed by the landers and their allies, especially the pods, who split into many angry swarmers when hit. Once all his humanoids have been abducted and then killed or mutated, the defender loses his planet and must face his enemies alone in space.

Fortunately, the player has several helpful devices to use. There are the scanner, which shows him where on the planet humanoids are being kidnapped; the smart bombs, which kill every enemy on the screen; and the HYPERSPACE button, which randomly moves the player to another spot on the screen (like the hyperspace in ASTEROIDS). Furthermore, on every fourth round, his planet and humanoids are replaced.

To the skilled player, no enemy is invincible. He must know when to shoot, when to move, and when to use smart bombs. He starts with only a few smart bombs, so he can use them only when absolutely necessary. The better he becomes, the more seldom he will need them, so he can save them for later in the game and use them then to score much higher.

The defender can carry one or more humanoids, setting them down when he wishes. As long as he carries at least one, though, he will never lose his planet. If he is confident that he can keep his ship through four rounds, he may want to keep one or two humanoids with him just for safety.

Game 2: PAC-MAN

The player maneuvers a circular yellow hero through a maze with the object of gobbling all the 240 dots and four "power capsules"; when one maze is completed, the next begins.

The game would be simple if not for the four monsters–Inky, Blinky, Pinky, and Clyde–who chase the Pac-Man continuously. A monster's eyes move in the direction it is traveling; it can "see" the Pac-Man when moving behind it. Each monster moves in a preset pattern until it sees the Pac-Man, and from then on it usually tracks him relentlessly, at each intersection turning onto the most direct route to him.

The Pac-Man must evade his pursuers at all costs. He can sometimes fool them with a "head fake," confusing them with several rapid reverses. When that fails, there are a few "safe spots" in each maze, a relative term, of course. Monsters always slow down when following him off the screen to the left or right. There is also an area above the monsters' centrally located pen in which it is easy for the Pac-Man to shake them. When he eats a power capsule, moreover, he can for a brief period earn points by catching them; then they turn blue and flee. After flashing four times, however, the monsters return to the chase.

The most successful players strive to earn bonus points as much as they do to complete screens, especially because later screens become much more difficult. Experienced players have developed patterns for evading the monsters for as long as possible each screen. Once the pursuit does begin, they know exactly when to eat a power capsule, catching a maximum number of monsters by surprise. The Pac-Man travels faster when not devouring dots, so it is best to save all four power capsules until the end of each screen, when a skilled monster-hunter can score most of his points. By adding only slight variations to his basic pattern, a Pac-Man veteran can go on for hundreds of screens.

Game 3: ASTEROIDS

The arcade version of ASTEROIDS operates on the same principles as the home version but with a few differences. The action moves faster, especially on machines that have been "enhanced." The hyperspace feature is there but not the flip or the shield, which appear in ASTEROIDS DELUXE. Both the asteroids and the ship are smaller in relation to the screen, and each medium-sized asteroid splits into two small ones, not one, when hit. Screens begin with a maximum of 16 asteroids instead of 8, which all break the way the "fast" ones do in the home version. When the last asteroid of a screen is destroyed, it takes a couple of seconds for the next one to appear.

The satellites are called large UFOs and fire just as randomly, but the small UFOs aim at the player's ship. Neither, fortunately, can shoot behind the screen. The player's ship still can, and it shoots in bursts of four, not two.

The most successful ASTEROIDS tactic, although it has allowed experts to play for over 50 hours, is impossible in the home version. It is called "lurking" or "hunting" and is considered unethical by some, and this is how it works: the player shoots all but one small or medium-sized asteroid. He then moves to the center of the screen and begins flying up over and over. As soon as any UFO appears, he turns and shoots. He is moving too fast for the UFO to track him, so he can take several shots, one of which is bound to hit. Since he earns a new ship with every 10,000 points, he can build up a tremendous stockpile with very little trouble; when he needs to take a break, he sacrifices just a few.

Instead of flying up the center again and again, certain players prefer to stay in one of the two top corners, about an inch from the side. The instant a UFO emerges from that side of the screen, they turn and zap it before it even has a chance to shoot. When one appears on the other side, they know how to shoot behind the screen with almost equal accuracy. Once either method of hunting is perfected, the game is reduced to a test of endurance.

Game 4: CENTIPEDE

CENTIPEDE is a very fast-moving game. The player's gun maneuvers in the bottom 3 inches or so of the playing field, shooting as many objects as it can. These objects include mushrooms dotting the screen, fleas falling straight down it, spiders zigzagging across the player's zone, scorpions crossing above it, and centipedes zigzagging down.

Each centipede has a head and from 0 to 11 body segments. It starts at the top and travels to the right until it hits a mushroom on the right edge, when it descends one level and starts traveling to the left, and so on. There are about 30 levels on the screen. When a centipede hits the bottom level of the player's zone, it starts traveling up in the same manner. The gun is destroyed on contact with any centipede or other bug, so it must shoot or avoid all of them. It is therefore undesirable to let a centipede reach the bottom because at that point the computer starts sending heads into the zone. Lone heads are the hardest centipedes to hit, so survival becomes increasingly difficult. As soon as the screen is clear of centipedes, however, replacements appear at the top.

The other creatures, each with its own sound effect, are also dangerous in their own ways. Fleas leave mushrooms behind them in the player's zone, producing a perilous clutter; erratic spiders do their best to hit the gun; and scorpions "poison" every mushroom they encounter. When a centipede hits a poisoned mushroom, it plummels to the bottom in a two-column zigzag, ignoring all mushrooms in its path and putting more pressure on the player.

Several basic tactics are essential to survival. The player must stay away from the edges whenever there is no spider on the screen, lest another suddenly appear. He must keep his zone clear of mushrooms, exterminate all centipedes as soon as possible, and avoid immediate dangers such as fleas and spiders.

Space considerations do not permit me to include the many minor but still vital observations and strategies for CENTIPEDE. As the game progresses, everything speeds up and becomes much harder, so the player has no choice but to forget the frills and to concentrate on the basics of survival.

Game 5: SCRAMBLE

The player pilots his jet along a "scrolling" terrain, that is, one that moves from right to left, giving the illusion that the stationary jet is flying from left to right. With his four-directional joystick, the player can maneuver the jet vertically and accelerate or decelerate it. There are also buttons for shooting lasers straight ahead and for dropping bombs in downward trajectories. Each round contains six sectors; although each sector is more difficult than the last, the rounds are all identical, making indefinite play possible. Each sector has its own threats and its own strategies; conquering all six means mastering the game.

Sector One is little more than a chance to score, since almost nothing menaces the jet in any way. The player can pick up points by hitting various targets clustered along the ground. Fuel tanks are especially valuable targets because they yield both points and fuel, which the jet needs for survival.

Sector Two is no different except for a swarm of evasive UFOs blocking the player's path. The player must shoot and maneuver his way through them.

In Sector Three, steering is more important than firing. Hordes of indestructible fireballs hurtle from right to left across the screen, traveling fast enough to make dodging them extremely risky even for the best players. The low hills at the bottom of the screen, however, provide cover for the jet. The trick is to destroy the targets in the valleys and to dart from valley to valley without hitting the fireballs that zoom every now and then just over the hilltops.

Once the player makes it through the fireballs, he encounters a series of tall buildings of various heights over which he must fly in a relatively narrow airspace. Targets of all kinds perch on rooftops, and rockets nestle in silos up to 2 inches deep. The jet must steer through even the narrowest passages cautiously in case a rocket takes off right under it.

Sector Five requires the most precise maneuvers of all. Horizontal passages, just wide enough to accommodate the jet, connect large caverns in which the player must fly all the way from top to bottom or back with very little horizontal room. To make matters worse, both the passages and the caverns can have rows of fuel tanks along the floor. If the jet tries to pass through these areas without shooting the fuel tanks in its path, it will crash.

In the final part of each round, the jet must make its way through a maze as treacherous as the last. At the bottom of every canyon over which the jet flies lies the base, a large octagon with flashing lights. The jet fires over canyon after canyon, using up fuel, until a base is destroyed. Unfortunately, the jet seems to fly too high to reach any base with lasers, and the canyons are too narrow for the use of bombs.

Many players do not realize that the jet is dispensable once the base is destroyed. In other words, once the jet has come close enough to the base to demolish it with a bomb or laser, it can crash against a wall and be replaced for free at the beginning of the next round.

Regarding the mastery of SCRAMBLE, one word of advice should suffice: memorize.

Game 6: PHOENIX

PHOENIX is reminiscent of Hitchcock's **The Birds.** Our feathered friends do their best to destroy us.

Each round consists of two warbird attacks, two phoenix attacks, and a battleship attack. The warbirds in the first two attacks appear in symmetrical formations from which they fall a few at a time to beleaguer the player with bombs. The surviving warbirds return to their places, where they use their little wings to walk from side to side.

The phoenixes, larger and quicker than warbirds, are not disabled by wing hits. They still swoop from side to side, slowing down at the edges but descending slightly with each crossing. The battleship descends slowly along with the alien it carries; only the alien's death can end the attack, but the alien is protected by the thick orange underside and revolving purple belt of the battleship, both of which must be shot through before the alien can perish. Moreover, the ship is defended by a formation of warbirds that fly just as in their own attacks, but they are shielded from the player's fire when in formation.

When the last warbird of the group is shot, the whole group is replaced.

The player has a shield that will destroy any bird it touches. It lasts for about 3 seconds, during which the ship can shoot but not move. Afterward, the shield cannot be used for approximately 5 seconds.

To exterminate an entire phoenix attack, players can move to a bottom corner and fire steadily, since the big birds are most vulnerable at the edges. Bombs from above are easily dodged, and ramming attempts from the side can be thwarted with the shield when it is used correctly.

I believe in shooting away the battleship's purple belt where it is exposed on the left or right. Since it is always moving, you must make many holes in it, then slide to the center and bore through the orange hull with rapid fire. The game becomes more difficult after the second round.

Game 7: GORF

GORF's five separate missions, several of them video games in their own right, are unusual. A voice synthesizer, challenging or complimenting the player, is another of its distinctive features. Also different is the multidirectional joystick, with its trigger. The player's ship can move anywhere within a block of space at the bottom of the screen; although it can move in an infinite number of directions and curves, it always points upward.

The trigger is no ordinary trigger. It fires a special "quark laser" with a new touch: the player has only one shot on the screen at a time, but **he** chooses which one. If he misses his target and doesn't want to wait for his shot to reach the top of the screen, all he has to do is press the trigger. Instantly, the first shot will disappear, and the next will be fired.

The first mission in each round, based on the game SPACE INVADERS, is relatively innocuous because there are only 24 invaders compared to 55 in each screen of the original game and 36 in the home version. The strategies are basically the same; the only new features are a cute Gorfian robot and a white shield in lieu of the usual shelters.

In the second mission, the enemy forces are centered around two laser cannons that fire every 2 or 3 seconds.They shift vertically and horizontally all over the screen, pulling their clusters of escorts with them. The escorts detach themselves one or two at a time and try to ram the player's ship from above without firing. The object of the mission is to destroy them and their cannons.

The next mission is similar to the game GALAXIANS (Game 8) except that there are 24 in each screen instead of 46, their bombs are not needles but pellets, and Gorfian robots hop across the top of the screen from time to time.

The fourth mission in each round features a black hole that releases spiraling spaceships and Gorfian robots that hurl meteorites at the player's ship. The attackers emerge one at a time, increasing in size until they destroy the ship, are destroyed themselves, or go off the edge.

The flagship mission ends each round. The flagship is a large, angular vessel with a nuclear reactor in its middle. It flies slowly from side to side near the top of the screen, descending each time and aiming diamond-shaped bombs at the player's ship. When the player shoots the nuclear reactor, he destroys the flagship and finishes the round.

As an unusual touch, the machine administers its own ranking system. Depending on how many rounds he completes, the player can be promoted from Space Cadet to Space Captain, Space Colonel, Space General, Space Warrior, or Space Avenger. Each round is harder than the last and each mission has its own secrets and strategies.

Game 8: GALAXIAN

Six rows of Galaxians float at the top of the screen, zigzagging enough to be hard to draw a bead on. Every so often, one from the extreme left or right of its row inverts and attacks. Dropping three or four bombs, it descends, sweeps across the screen, and then exits at the edge, only to reappear at the top and tumble into its original position. In later screens, up to five will attack at once.

The player must shoot as often as possible, being careful not to waste shots. He must learn the Galaxians' attack patterns, observing that each variety has its vulnerable point. Since Galaxians are worth twice as much when attacking, the player should try to shoot as many attackers as possible. (For more details, see **How To Master the Video Games.**)

Game 9: BERZERK

BERZERK is a paranoid's nightmare. The player-controlled humanoid runs through maze after maze filled with homicidal robots, all of which can shoot and move in eight directions. The robots track the humanoid and shoot at him at every opportunity. When the humanoid manages to shoot every robot in a maze, he receives a bonus.

The only other character is Evil Otto, a smiling ball that bounces after the humanoid and kills him on contact. Fortunately, Otto also vaporizes any robot in his path.

The player must not touch any wall or robot, and diagonal robot bullets are especially hard to dodge. The robots are, luckily, not too smart, so they frequently shoot each other or walk into the deadly walls. If the player cannot shoot all the robots himself, he can maneuver them through their tracking instincts. There are at least four ways in which he can engineer indirect deaths for them.

Still, BERZERK requires constant alertness and planning. From the second he enters each maze, the player must concentrate on exterminating robots, staying out of their lines of fire, and navigating his way through them. As the game progresses, moreover, Otto appears sooner in each maze and bounces more quickly.

Game 10: ASTEROIDS DELUXE

ASTEROIDS DELUXE differs from arcade ASTEROIDS in several respects. The former game allows a buildup of only ten extra ships. The large UFO ("satellite" in the home version) now shoots with deadly accuracy. Three out of every four shots are directed at asteroids; the fourth is directed at the player's ship. The small UFO is more lethal than ever. It shoots at asteroids only once for every two shots it takes at the player's ship.

The hexagonal death satellites pose a new threat. Each one drifts until hit, then splits into three diamonds, which try to ram the player's ship. Each diamond, when hit, splits into two wedges that rotate until they point to the player's ship and make even quicker beelines for it until they reach it or are destroyed.

The player's ship cannot go into hyperspace, but it does share a protective feature with its counterpart in the home version: the shield. A shielded ship cannot shoot, but it can rotate and thrust; the shield runs out after only a few seconds' use and can give way at any moment until it is recharged with the beginning of a new screen.

Because the UFOs now shoot deliberately, hunting is no longer effective. The player's targets are bound to shoot any asteroid he has spared, thus starting a dangerous new screen. The player should try, though, to save death satellites for later in each screen, when he has more free space in which to evade them. He must be prepared, though, for a death satellite to be shot prematurely by a UFO, producing two immediate threats at once.

12

APPENDIX: SOME OF THE MAJOR MANUFACTURERS

Activision, Inc.
3255-2 Scott Boulevard
Santa Clara, CA 95051
(408) 727-7770

APF Electronics, Inc.
1501 Broadway
New York, NY 10036
(212) 869-1960

Astrovision
6400 Busch Blvd., Suite 225
Columbus, OH 43229
(614) 885-0130

Atari, Inc.
1265 Borregas Ave.
Sunnyvale, CA 94086
(408) 745-2500

Coleco Industries, Inc.
945 Asylum Ave.
Hartford, CN 06105
(203) 278-0280

Imagic
20665 4th Street #244
Saratoga, CA 95070

Magnavox Consumer Elec. Corp.
P.O. Box 6950
Knoxville, TN 37914
(615) 521-4332

Mattel, Inc.
5150 Rosecrans Ave.
Hawthorne, CA 90250
(213) 978-5150

Zircon International, Inc. (Fairchild's distributor)
475 Vandell Way
Campbell, CA 95008
(408) 866-4500